Creative Bible Studies for Young Adults

By Denny Rydberg

Loveland, Colorado

Dedication

To my son, Josh.

Acknowledgments

I want to thank the members of the 1988-89 and
1989-90 University Ministries staff who contributed to this
book: Jim Allen, Connie McKeague Bernard, Sue Harris, Rod
Handley, Sue Jernberg, Doug Kuhn, Renee Lawler, Annette
Neelley, Lou Nemeth, Kim Ebeling Nollan, Dick Rant,
Chris Rogers and Marilyn Rydberg.

Creative Bible Studies for Young Adults
Copyright © 1990 by Denny Rydberg

Credits
Edited by Eugene C. Roehlkepartain
Designed by Judy Atwood Bienick
Cover design by Judy Atwood Bienick

Scripture quotations are from the Holy Bible, New International Version.
Copyright © 1973, 1978, 1984 by International Bible Society. Used by
permission of Zondervan Publishing House. All rights reserved.

Library of Congress Cataloging-in-Publication Data
Rydberg, Denny.
    Creative Bible studies for young adults / by Denny Rydberg.
        p.   cm.
        ISBN 0-931529-99-9
        1. Church group work with young adults. 2. Bible—Study.
3. Young adults—Religious life. I. Title.
BV4446.R93   1990
268'.434—dc20
                                                    90-32188
                                                    CIP

14 13 12 11 10 9 8 7 6   04 03 02 01 00 99 98 97 96 95
Printed in the United States of America.

Contents

Series 4: Discipleship and God's Will

Series 5: Growing in Faith

Satisfying a Spiritual Hunger

Christian young adults hunger for spiritual depth. They want to know what the Bible says and if what it says works in real life.

Away from home, they can no longer "borrow" their parents' faith; they have to discover a faith they can call their own. That involves asking tough questions, searching for answers and discovering how their faith affects their lives.

What's in the Book?

Creative Bible Studies for Young Adults seeks to meet young adults' need to explore scripture by letting scripture speak to five of young adults' key concerns:

- stress;
- sexuality;
- success;
- discipleship; and
- spiritual growth.

Each topic is addressed with a series of four meetings—giving you 20 studies in all. Each session is:

Young-adult-centered—Young adults (ages 18 to 35) are articulate and willing to share. These studies bring out participants' experiences and knowledge to enrich the study for everyone.

Group members are actively involved in each session. Their dialogue, interaction and participation make the studies come alive. The leader is a facilitator and guide—an important factor but not the all-knowing teacher with all the answers.

Application-centered—The studies center around the Bible and how it relates to class members' everyday lives and concerns. They move from "What does the Bible say?" to "How does this passage apply to our lives today?"

Christ- and Bible-centered—Ephesians 1:10 says God's plan is "to bring all things in heaven and on earth together under one head, even Christ." Christ clarifies the message. The Bible speaks it. These sessions seek to provide a format in which young adults listen to Christ through the Word.

Varied and creative—The studies in this book employ a variety of techniques that enhance learning and enjoyment. In addition to discussion questions, you'll find worksheets, games, simulations, small group activities and other approaches. These approaches will keep young adults interested and will help them remember what they've learned.

Flexible—These sessions can be used many different times—on Sunday mornings, Sunday nights or weekdays. They can be used as content for a retreat. They can be amplified and expanded.

The length is also flexible. The sessions each should take between 45 minutes and an hour. But they can be expanded by spending more time in discussion. Or they can be cut by deleting activities.

Use one series one month and another series two months later. Choose the topics that fit your young adults at a particular time. Make the series work for you.

Easy to use—The programs are easy to use and don't require much preparation. For most, you just have to read the appropriate scripture passages, gather a few supplies and photocopy handouts. And you're ready!

You don't have to be an experienced leader to lead these sessions. The outlines are simple and clear. So relax. These sessions are easy enough for any adult to lead. And they're great for self-led young adult groups.

How the Sessions Are Arranged

The Bible studies are set up in an easy-to-follow format. After a brief introduction to the topic, you'll find these sections:

Surveying the Session—The session's learning objectives.

Understanding the Word—A brief overview of the biblical background for the session.

Preparing to Lead—What you need to prepare for the session, including supplies to gather.

Starting the Session—An opening activity that grabs attention and helps move into the topic.

Digging Into the Word—The "meat" of the study, which guides students to explore the scripture and its meaning.

Applying the Word—Questions and activities to help young adults apply the passage to their lives.

Affirming Each Other—Activities that build community and affirm participants in ways that relate to the session's topic.

Closing the Session—A wrap-up for the session that often includes prayer or some kind of commitment.

I believe these studies will help young adults discover answers to many questions they're asking. And I pray that participants will encourage each other to live with integrity because of what they've learned.

God bless you as you explore these studies together.

TIPS FOR LEADING YOUNG ADULTS

If you don't have much experience leading young adults, don't worry. Just follow these 11 tips for effective Bible studies.

1. Enjoy yourself. Leading a Bible study is a great way to enjoy personal Bible study even more. And your enjoyment and interest will be contagious as you lead others to study.

2. Enjoy your group. Young adults are fun and challenging to hang out with. They have energy, intelligence, openness and questions. They're making crucial choices in life. They can be challenged to serve God with vigor. What a privilege to minister to and with young adults!

3. Don't call them young adults to their faces. You can call the group the "young adult group," although with some creativity you'd probably discover a better title. And you can refer to "young adults" when you're talking to older adults. But when you're talking to young adults, just call them adults. After all, we don't call people in their 40s "older adults" or people in their 60s "very old adults."

4. Concentrate on relationships before content. Get to know the people. Be involved in their lives beyond the classroom. Good relationships lead to better Bible study, since people will open up and be honest when they've developed relationships.

5. **Remember that all adults aren't good readers.** Some are as embarrassed to read aloud as they were as kids when their teachers called on them. Always ask for volunteers when you want something read aloud.

6. **Emphasize group participation.** See yourself as the guide, not the almighty instructor delivering the equivalent of the Ten Commandments. Use a light touch so participants will respond openly.

7. **Create an environment for sharing.** For discussions, sit in a circle so people can see each other. Have coffee and snacks to add to the informality.

8. **Include everyone.** Be sure some people don't dominate discussions when others have something to say. Make sure everyone has a Bible and other materials needed for the study.

9. **Affirm often.** Thank those who share ideas—even if you thought the idea was a loser. Encourage and support group members as they ask questions and apply what they're learning to their lives.

10. **Don't expect too much too soon.** If the group hasn't had much experience in participatory Bible study, it might take time for them to feel comfortable sharing. Stay with them. Encourage them to gradually open up.

11. **Pray.** Immerse your preparation and leadership in prayer. Pray for the participants in your group. And pray that the study will help people grow in their faith.

SERIES 1

HANDLING STRESS

"**T**he Heat Is On." That was the theme song for Eddie Murphy's movie, *Beverly Hills Cop.*

It could also be the theme song for many young adults' lives. They feel like they're in a pressure cooker that's about to explode. Burned out. Tired out. Worn out. Stressed out.

Sometimes, ready to bail out.

Stress comes with the territory in the '90s. It wears on you and makes you tense. It may also make you eat less or more, and—in the process—you can become irritable or even sick. You can become self-absorbed and isolated.

Is that how God wants us to live? On the edge, adrenalin pumping, face screwed on tight, waiting for a less-stressed future—only to find ourselves burned out in the meantime.

Is the Bible contemporary enough to help us cope with this fast-paced life?

Stress isn't new. More than 2,500 years ago, Daniel—a young man, probably in his late teens—faced stress. He'd been uprooted from his home and dumped into foreign territory. His life involved one stressful situation after another.

That's what this four-session series is about: handling stress from a biblical perspective. We'll see what we can learn from Daniel and the Lord about dealing with this difficult issue. The sessions focus on these issues:

● **Stress 1**—Concrete principles for dealing with the stress of change;

● **Stress 2**—How to handle the stress of an impossible task;

● **Stress 3**—What do to when you're being pushed to compromise your beliefs; and

● **Stress 4**—Biblical principles for coping with and reducing stress.

New Places, New Stresses

A study reported in American Demographics magazine found that young adults are more likely to move than any other age group. The median age of people who move five or more times in three years is 24.

Moving epitomizes the changes young adults experience. In fact, just about the only thing that's consistent for young adults is change. Things change constantly for young adults. They move. They go to new schools. They get new jobs.

And whether the changes they experience are anticipated or dreaded, they create stress. The stress of being in unfamiliar settings. The stress of having new responsibilities. The stress of being with different people.

In Daniel 1, Daniel faced similar changes as a young adult: new work, new surrounding and new culture. Yet he handled the stress well and was eventually promoted as an influential leader in Babylon— the most powerful nation of his time.

Though Daniel lived about 600 years before Christ, his model of coping with stressful change has valuable lessons for young adults today.

SURVEYING THE SESSION

This session looks to Daniel's example to discover concrete principles for dealing with the stress of change. Young adults will:
- share their experiences of change;
- study the stresses Daniel faced when his whole world changed;
- discover principles for coping with stress and change;

- affirm each other for giving support in stressful times; and
- commit to focusing on a new way to cope effectively with stress.

UNDERSTANDING THE WORD

Scripture focus—Daniel 1:1-21.

In 605 B.C., Babylonian King Nebuchadnezzar defeated Judah, besieged Jerusalem and carried treasures and people back to his homeland as war plunder. One of those people was Daniel.

The first six chapters of Daniel tell how Daniel and his fellow Israelites faced pressure to give up their faith and worship other gods. In chapter 1, Daniel felt pressure to abandon Jewish dietary laws to eat the king's bountiful feast—food offered to idols and ceremonially unclean.

Daniel resisted the pressure, and in the process, taught a great deal about coping with change and stress.

PREPARING TO LEAD

Before the session, study Daniel 1:1-21. Then read the entire session outline. Make sure all the activities fit your group, and make any necessary changes.

Gather the materials for the session. You'll need national and world maps, masking tape, newsprint, a marker and several pads of Post-it notes. For each person you'll need a Bible, a pen or pencil, a copy of "The More Things Change . . . " handout (page 18), two or three rubber bands, a 3×5 card and a straight pin.

STARTING THE SESSION

Post the national and world maps in your meeting room and arrange chairs to face the maps. When everyone has arrived, welcome participants and have them each answer each of the following questions before you ask the next one.

As students are answering the questions, interrupt every minute or so and have everyone get up and switch seats.

Ask these questions:

● **Where are three places you've lived?** (Have students point out the places on a map.)

● **What did you like and dislike about each place?**

● **When in your life have you experienced the most transition and change? How did you feel about the changes?**

When all students have answered all questions, ask:

● **How did it feel to move around so much during the discussion? Was it irritating? annoying? disconcerting?**

● **How is this simulation like the changes we experience in life?**

DIGGING INTO THE WORD

Explain that this session is about the stress of change. It's a stress Daniel faced to an extreme and learned to deal with. Give some background information on the story. Use the Understanding the Word section as a guide. Then have someone read aloud Daniel 1:1-21.

Form four groups, and give each group a "The More Things Change ..." handout (page 18). A group can be a pair or an individual. Have groups discuss the questions and be ready to report.

When groups have finished discussing, have them report what they learned. Then brainstorm and list on a sheet of newsprint all the types of stress Daniel may have experienced in those 21 verses.

Ask:

● **Have you ever felt besieged? What emotions welled up inside you?**

● **Do you sometimes feel like you're in foreign territory? If so, what pressures do you feel that cause stress?**

● **If you were carried off to a foreign land, what would you think or worry about?**

● **When have you felt like you were being evaluated like Daniel was evaluated?**

● **What has been one of the toughest requests you've had to ask of an employer, teacher or parent? How'd you prepare yourself to make the request? What happened? What was God's role in your request?**

 ## APPLYING THE WORD

Go back to the list of Daniel's stresses you created. Check the stress points young adults still experience. Add other stresses class members face.

Say: **Stress is caused often by a change in location, a different culture or a new job.**

Then ask:

● **What's a new situation for you right now? What stress do you feel because of this change?**

● **Do you sometimes feel like a stranger in a strange land? How do you cope?**

● **What's causing the most stress for you right now? How well are you coping with that stress?**

Lay the list of stresses on a table or the floor in the middle of your class. Give each student a pencil and several Post-it notes. If Post-it notes aren't available, use 3×5 cards and tape.

Have class members think of principles and ideas for dealing with the stress of change. Have them write their ideas on a Post-it note, read it aloud and stick it on top of the list of stresses. Encourage people to share ways they've dealt with stresses they've encountered.

Have young adults continue sticking Post-it notes until most of the newsprint is covered. Then say: **These notes give us lots of ideas of how to cope with stress and change. The notes don't get rid of the stress—just like our coping techniques don't get rid of the stress. Rather, they focus our energies on positive responses to the stress instead of just fretting about it.**

Have each class member choose one of the coping ideas to take home and use as a reminder to cope effectively with stress.

 ## AFFIRMING EACH OTHER

Point out how much participants learned from each other in the previous activity. Then say: **Sometimes we may feel alone in coping with stress and change. But just as Daniel had his friends, there are Christian friends beside us to support and encourage us in the midst of stress and change.**

Give each young adult two or three rubber bands. Ask them to give each rubber band to someone in the class who has eased some of the pressure they've felt when they were about to "snap." Have them share their experience with the whole group. Watch for people who don't get rubber bands, and affirm them yourself.

Also ask people to mail a rubber band and a short note of encouragement to a friend in the next week as an affirmation.

 ## CLOSING THE SESSION

Remind class members of how the king changed the Hebrews' names when they went to Babylon. Then have class members remember times when God changed names. Some examples include:
- Abram to Abraham;
- Jacob to Israel; and
- Simon to Peter.

Give class members each a pen or pencil, a 3×5 card and a straight pin. On one side of the card, have them write a name that describes how they sometimes fail to cope well with change and stress. For example, they could write Fearful Frank or Paranoid Patricia. Have people each pin on their name tag and explain what they wrote.

Say: **All of us have trouble coping with stress sometimes. But we can apply what we've learned from the Bible**

**and each other today to cope more effectively when stress
and change come.**

Have people take off their name tags. On the other side,
have them write a new name they can take that symbolizes their
new commitment to learning to cope with stress and change.
For example, they could write Faithful Frank or Peaceful Patricia.
Have young adults share what they wrote.

Form pairs. If you have an extra person, form one trio.
Have people each pray for their partner that he or she will learn
to rely on God to help through times of stress and change. Form
a large circle and join hands. Pray that each person will support
others as they seek to have Daniel's strength and perseverance
in the coming week.

Encourage group members to keep a stress journal for the
rest of the series on stress. Three or four times each week, have
them write what stresses and changes they're facing and how
they're responding to them. Suggest they include lessons God is
teaching them in the midst of the changes.

THE MORE THINGS CHANGE . . .

Group #1—Read and discuss Daniel 1:1-2.

1. Define "besieged." What stresses would you feel if you were besieged? What would you think about? What would the future look like to you?

2. What's the significance of verse 2? What's your reaction to the sentence, "And the Lord delivered Jehoiakim king of Judah into his hand"?

3. What characteristic of God does the statement demonstrate? How does this characteristic relate to handling stress?

Group #2—Read and discuss Daniel 1:3-7.

1. The first part of verse 4 sounds like a "meat market" or audition. What might Daniel have felt in this scene?

2. What was the point of the king's order? What did the king want to get out of it?

3. What was the significance of the name changes in verse 7?

Group #3—Read and discuss Daniel 1:8-14.

1. What was the significance of the dietary laws Daniel was being told to break?

2. What stress might Daniel have felt when he was told to break his dietary laws? What additional stress would be created by Daniel asking to keep the dietary laws?

3. Does the test Daniel set up seem like a good way to get the official's permission?

Group #4—Read and discuss Daniel 1:15-21.

1. How did Daniel's test turn out? What was the payoff?

2. What was God's part and what was Daniel's part in this story?

3. What did Daniel need to do? What did God need to do? How did God help Daniel in doing his part?

The Impossible Dream

"**I**'ll never get this paper finished."

"This assignment is impossible."

"How does my boss expect me to do this on time?"

"I just don't have time to do everything."

Young adults live in a challenging world. They face dozens of demands from professors, parents, employers, friends, spouses and themselves. They may feel crushed under the burden of new responsibilities, overwhelming tasks and unrealistic expectations.

It's all a recipe for stress.

Once again, Daniel's story parallels the pressures young adults feel. Though he was victorious and successful in chapter 1, Daniel still faced living under the rule of absolute despots who governed by whims. His life was plagued with unpredictable events and impossible tasks.

His next challenge came when the king had a dream that he wanted his advisers—including Daniel—to tell him about and interpret. The task seemed impossible, yet the consequence of not accomplishing the task would be death. So Daniel's stress continued.

But he learned to cope with it and meet the challenges before him. As in Session 1, we can learn from Daniel.

SURVEYING THE SESSION

This session helps young adults discover how Daniel faced the stress of the impossible task. Young adults will:

- participate in an earthquake simulation that explores how people cope with impossible tasks;
- develop newscasts that describe Daniel's challenge;
- find in the passage skills for coping with impossible tasks;
- create collages to symbolize challenges they face;

● affirm strengths in each other; and
● pray that God will help them through their challenges.

UNDERSTANDING THE WORD

Scripture focus—Daniel 2:1-49.

This chapter tells the famous story of Nebuchadnezzar's dream. Though it was common for astrologers to interpret a king's dream in Babylon, the king wouldn't tell them what he dreamed. Instead, he wanted the astrologers to tell him what he dreamed and what it meant—a seemingly impossible order. Adding to the drama, he became furious that they couldn't do it and ordered they be executed.

Daniel intervened on behalf of the astrologers and, through prayer, was able to fulfill the king's command. Daniel told of a dream that predicted the eventual downfall of the Babylonian empire. The king saw God's power and fell down in worship.

PREPARING TO LEAD

Before the session, study Daniel 2:1-49. Then read the entire session outline. Make sure all the activities fit your group, and make any necessary changes.

Gather materials for the session. You'll need newsprint, markers, old magazines, glue, construction paper and scissors. For each person you'll need a Bible, a copy of "The Impossible Task" handout (page 24), and a pen or pencil.

STARTING THE SESSION

Welcome students to the session. Informally ask about how the stress journal has gone for them since the first session. Ask what insights they've gained.

If you have more than 12 people, form groups of six to eight. Then introduce the simulation experience.

Say: **Here's our predicament: This building has just
been struck by an earthquake. Debris is everywhere. You're
trapped in the room, and there's only one small escape
route. Aftershocks will begin any minute. And when that
happens, those who remain will certainly die. All but three
people will be able to escape.**

Who'll leave? And who'll stay to face certain death?

**How'll you select the three who'll stay? Of those who'll
escape, who's first priority for departure? Have people line
up their chairs in order of escape—just in case the
aftershocks come sooner and fewer people escape.**

Allow the group time to make choices.

Then ask:

● **What feelings did you have when I described the
situation?**

● **How did you feel when you were selected to stay or
leave? Did you feel worthy? unworthy? unfairly treated?
Why?**

● **What was most difficult about the assignment?**

● **When in your life have you been given similarly
difficult tasks?**

● **How did you feel during the time leading up to and
during the task? afterward? What did you learn from it?**

 # DIGGING INTO THE WORD

Say: **Daniel also faced some seemingly impossible
tasks while in exile in Babylon. Daniel 2 describes one of
those tasks: interpreting King Nebuchadnezzar's dream.**

Form groups of about four. If your class has six or fewer
students, stay as one group. Have someone in each group read
aloud Daniel 2:1-13. Then have the group develop a two-minute
TV "news bite" about the 13 verses. They may use live reports,
interviews, commentaries—whatever they like. After five to eight
minutes, have each group present its newscast.

Then ask:

● **What stress would Daniel feel if he read verse 13?**

● **If you were in Daniel's place, what would you think
about the situation in these verses?**

Read aloud Daniel 2:14-19. Say: **Daniel showed great**

wisdom in dealing with his situation. He avoided panic, and used at least four steps to deal with the stress of an impossible task.

Have class members identify the four steps, and write them on newsprint. If someone sees other steps, include them too. The steps are:

1. He speaks with wisdom and tact, and gets the information.

2. He asks for more time.

3. He gets the support and counsel of friends.

4. He praises God.

 ## APPLYING THE WORD

Form pairs. If you have an extra person, form one trio. Give each person "The Impossible Task" handout (page 24), and a pen or pencil. Have each pair work together on the handout. Then bring the group together in a circle to discuss what students learned that was significant to them.

Place old magazines, glue, markers, construction paper and scissors in the center of your group and have students each create a collage that represents an impossible task they're facing right now.

Have volunteers each share their artistic expression.

Then ask:

● **What have you learned from Daniel about how you can approach this impossible task?**

● **What other insights have you gained in the past that'll help you with this task?**

 ## AFFIRMING EACH OTHER

Have people each pass their collage around the circle. On the back of each collage, have people each write something they see in the person whose collage they have that will help that person meet the challenge of an overwhelming task. For example, someone might write, "You have incredible persistence" or "You have an inner peace that'll see you through."

CLOSING THE SESSION

When the collages have gone all the way around the circle, give people time to read what others wrote and to make any comments that seem appropriate to them.

Then have people each pass their collage to the person on the right. Go around the circle, and have each person pray for the person whose collage they hold. Ask them to thank God for that person's gifts, and to pray that the person will find the strength to meet the challenges he or she faces.

Ask class members each to put their collage in their journal. Encourage them to write journal entries in the coming week that relate to how God is helping them deal with seemingly impossible tasks.

THE IMPOSSIBLE TASK

1. Read Daniel 2:19-23. What's the payoff in verse 19? What's Daniel's response to that gift?

2. What do you learn about God from Daniel's song? Based on the song, how does God ease stress in the lives of believers?

3. Read Daniel 2:24-28. How does Daniel handle the information he was given in the dream? What personality traits does this response reveal in Daniel? Did those traits help or hurt him when faced with stress?

4. Read Daniel 2:46-49. If Daniel had not faced this stressful situation, what would Nebuchadnezzar have missed learning? What about Daniel?

5. How would Daniel's new position add to or relieve stress?

6. Do you think life ever becomes stress-free? Explain. How does your view shape your response to stressful situations?

Feeling the Heat

Fudge the figures. Give the answers. Cover up the truth.

Young adults feel pressure from all sides to compromise what they believe. It could be a boss who asks them to do something illegal. It could be a classmate who asks them to "help" with a test. It could be a friend who asks them to go to a drinking party.

Whatever the source, the stress is the same. You could lose a friend. Or a promotion. Or a grade. Or a job.

The stress in Daniel 3 was similar but even greater. Daniel's friends, Shadrach, Meshach and Abednego, didn't just risk a friendship or a job; they risked their lives by not giving into the pressure to compromise their faith. King Nebuchadnezzar and his pride forced Daniel's buddies under the heat of the moment and into the heat of a fiery furnace.

SURVEYING THE SESSION

This session helps young adults learn to stand up to the pressure to compromise what they believe. Young adults will:
- uncover and discuss the stresses in Daniel 3;
- identify times they feel under pressure to compromise their beliefs;
- affirm the importance of Christian friends;
- share one area where they "feel the heat" to compromise; and
- discover how God can help keep them cool.

UNDERSTANDING THE WORD

Scripture focus—Daniel 3:1-30.

Daniel doesn't appear in Daniel 3, but his "co-stars"—King

Nebuchadnezzar and Señor Stress—remain central characters.

This passage tells about the king's edict that all citizens bow down and worship a 90-foot golden statue. But Shadrach, Meshach and Abednego—three faithful Israelites who were leaders in Babylon—refused.

The king's astrologers told him of the disobedience, and in his anger he threw them into the furnace. The story of their miraculous escape is one of the most vivid in the Old Testament. While they were in the furnace, the king saw a fourth person with them—an angel of God. The king then recognized God's power and decreed that all the people worship this God.

 # PREPARING TO LEAD

Before the session, study Daniel 3:1-30. Then read the entire session outline. Make sure all the activities fit your group, and make any necessary changes.

Gather materials for the session. You'll need a candle, a box of matches, newsprint, masking tape and a glass of water. For each person you'll need a marker, a wooden block or blank cardboard box, a red pen or pencil, a Bible and a copy of "The Heat's On" handout (page 30).

 # STARTING THE SESSION

Welcome everyone. Talk informally about the stress journals.

Form a circle, and light a candle.

Ask:

● **What's your most vivid memory of fire? It can be a happy, sad or tragic memory.**

Answer the question for yourself, then pass the candle to someone, and have him or her recall a memory. Continue passing the candle until all have shared.

DIGGING INTO THE WORD

Form a circle, and read aloud Daniel 3:1-7. Then give people each a marker, and a small wooden block or blank cardboard box. Have young adults each write on their block all the stresses they perceive in the passage. Then have them each stack their block in the middle of the group as they describe the stresses.

Next, read aloud Daniel 3:8-12.

Ask:

● **What motivated the astrologers in this passage? jealousy? racism? prejudice? something else?**

● **When have you experienced jealousy or prejudice? What stress did you feel?**

● **When have you been jealous or prejudiced toward someone or a group? What stress did you see in that person or group?**

Form pairs. If you have an extra person, form one trio. Give people each a red pen or pencil, and a copy of "The Heat's On" handout (page 30) to complete.

When they've all finished, ask:

● **What factors made the most difference in the stress level for Shadrach, Meshach and Abednego? for King Nebuchadnezzar?**

● **What do those differences tell you about handling the stress of being told to go against what you believe?**

● **What other insights did you gain from the passage?**

APPLYING THE WORD

Write the following headings each on separate sheets of newsprint: Home, School, Work, Personal Relationships, Public Life, Private Life, Family, Other. Tape the sheets to the walls.

Give people each a marker, and have them go around and write times they've "felt the heat" to compromise in each area. For example, a student might've felt the need to stifle his or her beliefs in a class. Or an employee might've felt pressure to produce something too quickly when he or she was concerned with quality control.

As a group, briefly focus on each sheet and ask:

● **Is this an area where you often feel the heat to compromise what you believe? If so, what pressures do you feel the most?**

● **How have you handled the stresses in this area?**

● **How has your relationship to God affected your ability to deal with stress? What have you learned in the process?**

● **Do you have the fourth person in your furnace? How have you seen evidence of him?**

 ## AFFIRMING EACH OTHER

Ask:

● **How important was it for Shadrach, Meshach and Abednego to have each other when they faced their temptation and endured their fiery trial?**

● **How do your friends support and encourage you when you feel the heat to go against your beliefs?**

Do a "cinnamon roll" hug to illustrate the need to support one another. Have people stand side by side in a straight line with arms around each other's shoulders. Then have the person at one end begin to "roll" into the group with his or her arm still around the next person. Continue until the whole group is rolled up like a cinnamon roll. When the roll is complete, have everyone squeeze. Unroll, and reverse the process so the person on the outside last time is on the inside this time.

 ## CLOSING THE SESSION

Form a circle, and place a glass of water in the middle. Say: **At times we all feel the heat to do things that go against what we believe. But our faith in God and his presence with us can keep us cool under pressure.**

I'm going to pass around a box of matches. When it

comes to you, take out a match, light it and say one area where you're particularly feeling the heat right now. Then before the match burns your fingers, dip it in the water. Say how you'll rely on God to keep you cool under that pressure.

Then take a match and begin the process yourself. Go around the circle. When everyone has shared, join hands and close with prayer.

Encourage people to pray for each other and to write in their stress journals through the week.

THE HEAT'S ON

1. Read Daniel 3:13-16. What would it feel like to have the king talk to you the way he talked to Shadrach, Meshach and Abednego? How would you likely respond?

2. Did the three know they'd be saved? Was being saved most important? Or was being faithful to God more important?

3. Read the conclusion of the story in Daniel 3:19-30. What gets the king's attention? What does he learn?

4. In the thermometers below, raise the temperature to indicate the stress level of the characters at each point in the story.

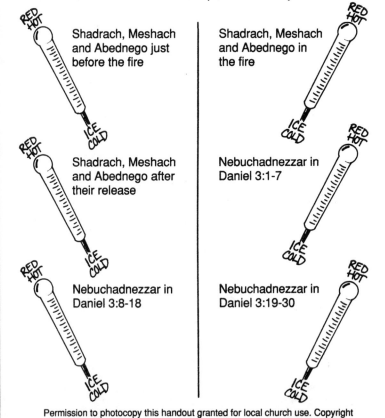

Shadrach, Meshach and Abednego just before the fire

Shadrach, Meshach and Abednego in the fire

Shadrach, Meshach and Abednego after their release

Nebuchadnezzar in Daniel 3:1-7

Nebuchadnezzar in Daniel 3:8-18

Nebuchadnezzar in Daniel 3:19-30

Solace Amid the Stress

Being stressed and burned out are not absolutes in life. A person doesn't have to succumb to stress even if everyone around him or her is. We can reduce the stress in our lives through some practical advice from the Bible.

In studying Daniel's life, we learned some things about reducing stress. But 65 other books in the Bible also talk about this subject. In this final study, we'll examine what other passages say about reducing stress in our lives.

SURVEYING THE SESSION

This final session in the series on stress explores ways to reduce stress. Young adults will:
- enact a TV talk show that explores different ways people advocate dealing with stress;
- participate in learning centers to discover Bible passages with advice for reducing stress;
- analyze and discuss stressful areas in their own lives;
- encourage each other to overcome stresses; and
- ask God to help them cope with a major stress they're experiencing.

UNDERSTANDING THE WORD

Scripture focus—Deuteronomy 6:3, 10-19; Colossians 3:13; 1 Thessalonians 5:16-18; and Hebrews 12:15.

This session moves outside the book of Daniel to examine a variety of scripture passages that give clues to reducing stress. The Deuteronomy passage focuses on the importance of obedience to God, emphasizing that following God is the key to life.

Colossians 3:13 deals with the importance of forgiving each other and caring for each other. The Thessalonian passage urges Christians to be joyful, prayerful and thankful. And Hebrews 12:15 warns against bitterness that causes trouble and stress.

 ## PREPARING TO LEAD

Before the session, study the passages listed in the Understanding the Word section. Then read the entire session outline. Make sure all the activities fit your group, and make any necessary changes.

Gather the materials for the session. You'll need five copies of the "Talk Show Personalities" handout (page 36). For each person you'll need a pen or pencil, and a copy of the "Measuring Your Stress" handout (page 39).

Prepare the learning centers for the Digging Into the Word section. Photocopy and cut apart the "Biblical Stress-Reducers" handout (page 37). Place each set of instructions on a separate table. Have a Bible at each center. Put supplies at the centers as follows:

● Learning Center #1—Put two simple children's puzzles on the table—taken apart. Have one puzzle upside down and the other right side up.

● Learning Center #2—No special materials are required.

● Learning Center #3—Have a full pitcher of water, three empty glasses, a teaspoon and a bottle of vinegar. If a sink isn't handy, have a bucket in which groups can pour water.

 ## STARTING THE SESSION

Welcome everyone to the final study in the series. Ask how the journaling has been going and if any new insights have been learned.

Then select five volunteers to perform a short skit. Give them each a copy of the "Talk Show Personalities" handout (page

36), which explains their roles. Enthusiastically introduce the show by saying: **Welcome to The Phil Winfrey Show! Today we have four national experts here to tell us how to successfully squelch stress. Here's your host—Phil Winfrey!**

Encourage the five volunteers to ham up their roles. Have Phil Winfrey take questions and comments from the audience. Don't let the skit go too long, but enjoy the caricatures.

After the skit, ask:

● **Which points made by the guests had merit? Which didn't?**

● **What suggestions seemed flaky or trite?**

● **Which suggestions seemed harmful or dangerous?**

● **If you were asked for advice on how to minimize stress and maximize meaning in life, what advice would you give?**

 # DIGGING INTO THE WORD

Say: **After three weeks of learning from Daniel how to handle stress, we'll look at some other biblical passages that can help us combat stress.**

Form three teams, and have each team begin working at different learning centers, which are described in the Preparing to Lead section. Have teams rotate centers every five to eight minutes.

When teams have each finished all three centers, bring the whole group together.

Ask:

● **What was the most important insight you gained from the activity?**

● **What other biblical advice would you give to reduce stress in life?**

 # APPLYING THE WORD

Give people each a pen or pencil, and a copy of the "Measuring Your Stress" handout (page 39) to complete on their own.

Then have people briefly share their cardiographs' significant points.

When everyone has shared, ask:

● **What did you learn about yourself from working on this graph?**

● **How would you characterize your life and stress level right now? a quiet pool? a gentle bay with waters lapping on the shore? a river with rapids in it? a raging torrent with a huge waterfall ahead?**

Have people choose one and explain.

● **What area of life causes you the most stress right now?**

● **Which biblical stress-reducer would particularly help you right now?**

 **AFFIRMING EACH OTHER**

Form a circle, then have people each share their biggest stress concern and how they plan to deal with it. Then have each person receive a "gift" from one other person that relates to that person's major stress.

For instance, suppose Kevin says his primary stress is the hurt he continually feels because of a broken relationship. He intends to practice forgiveness and break out of his self-imposed cocoon. Someone might say to Kevin: "Kevin, I give you the gift of the healing of memories and the freedom to leave your cocoon and fly like a butterfly. And I want you to know I'll be praying for you."

Continue until everyone has given and received a gift.

 **CLOSING THE SESSION**

To close the session, read Matthew 11:28-30. Say: **Our stresses can consume us if we let them. But if we ask Jesus to share our load, it becomes more manageable. And when we're yoked together with Jesus, we're obedient in following him.**

Draw a yoke on news-
print (see sample in adjacent
box) and have markers
available. Have people all
bow their heads in silent
prayer. Then as they feel
comfortable, have people
each go to the newsprint
and write a stress they'll give
to Jesus.

When everyone who
wants to write something
has finished, form a huddle with people reaching into the center
to join hands. Pray that God will give people the strength to
cope with the stresses they face.

TALK SHOW PERSONALITIES

Phil Winfrey—A typical talk show host, who has the best and worst characteristics of famous media personalities.

Werner Earwig—Werner practices New Age concepts. Meditation is the key, and personal fulfillment is the goal. Werner uses New Age buzzwords and phrases: "Get in touch with yourself," "Discover the real you," "Let go, and let your true self emerge," "Don't get hung up on the rules of religion."

Jane Hardbody—Jane is a fitness freak. She teaches aerobics, manages a health club, and owns a natural food and vitamin store. She believes if you get in shape and eat the right foods, you'll look and feel good, and have the energy and outlook to handle stress much better. What's more, you'll burn off your frustrations by working out.

Dr. Tom Pharmaceutical—A medical doctor, Tom believes drugs are the key to combating stress. He doesn't think you should overuse drugs, but a little Valium goes a long way. He also suggests you watch your blood pressure and cholesterol—and see him every six months.

Rev. Dr. C. Wallace Medley—Rev. Medley, a pious preacher, preaches that Jesus is the answer, but Rev. Medley's not sure of the questions. The Bible answers the stress issues of our time. If people followed the Word, they wouldn't experience stress. So naturally, stress is a sign of sin.

BIBLICAL STRESS-REDUCERS

Learning Center #1—Obedience

Form two groups. One group must put together the puzzle with the picture showing. The other group must put together the upside-down puzzle without looking at the front. See which group finishes first.

Discuss these questions:

● Which puzzle was easier to put together? Why?

● What happens to our stress when we don't follow instructions?

● How can following instructions reduce stress? Give examples.

Read Deuteronomy 6:3, 10-19.

Then discuss:

● What's the promise of obedience? disobedience?

● Why does obedience reduce stress?

● When has disobedience to God raised or lowered your stress level?

Take apart the puzzles before leaving this learning center.

Learning Center #2—Joy, Thanks and Prayer

Read 1 Thessalonians 5:16-18.

Discuss these questions:

● Do these three commands—to always be joyful, prayerful and grateful—seem easy or impossible to follow? Explain.

● How are the three commands interconnected?

● If you could follow these three commands, how would they affect your stress level?

● What experiences have you had with these commands?

continued

Learning Center #3—Forgiveness

Pour a fresh glass of water, and have each person take a sip. Then add about a teaspoon of vinegar. Have each person take a sip. Then pour out half the mixture and add more water. Can people still taste the vinegar?

Discuss:

● Which taste is more dominant—the water or the vinegar?

● What would it take to get rid of the vinegar taste in the water?

● How is the vinegar in the water like having a bitter attitude in life?

Read Hebrews 12:15.

Discuss:

● How does bitterness affect our lives?

Read Colossians 3:13.

Discuss:

● How does forgiveness dissipate bitterness?

● How would a spirit of forgiveness reduce stress?

MEASURING YOUR STRESS

On the cardiograph below, plot the past month in your life as follows:

- Mark exciting things high on the chart.
- Mark depressing, negative things low on the chart.
- Mark normal, stress-free things along the middle.

Therefore, if the last month was relatively calm and stress-free, your line would line up mostly in the middle. If you've had a lot of highs and lows, your line would go up and down on the chart.

Mark significant events such as tests, job interviews, deadlines and relaxing weekends where they apply. Note any particular resources that helped you deal with the stresses you experienced.

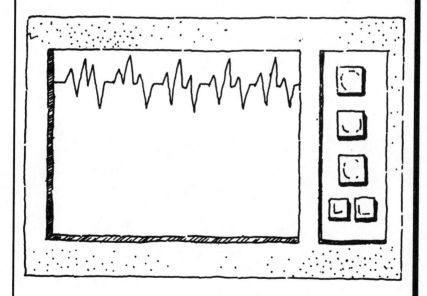

SEX: GOD'S GOOD IDEA

Christian young adults are trapped in the aftershocks of the sexual revolution. The world sends mixed messages about sex. Some people say, "If it feels good, do it." Others retort, "If it feels good, it's probably sinful."

What's right? What's wrong? Who can they listen to?

In *Clear-Headed Choices in a Sexually-Confused World* (Group Books), Terry Hershey writes: "Today's young adults are having more trouble with relationships than almost any other area of their lives. They're afraid of commitment, and they're confused by the number of choices they face."

In the midst of our sexual confusion and the mixed messages, we need to seek God's perspective on this volatile subject. Otherwise, we're likely to fall into two opposite traps. On the one hand, we can believe sex is trivial and common-place—something to titillate but nothing too special. Or on the other hand, we can come to think of sex as vulgar, dirty and profane—something to be eliminated from films, magazines, conversation and culture.

What then is the proper perspective? This four-session series reminds us that sex was God's idea in the first place. It's a good gift to be used responsibly. The sessions focus on these issues:

- **Sex 1**—What God originally intended sex to be;
- **Sex 2**—How sex can be distorted to become sinful;
- **Sex 3**—Sex in singleness and marriage; and
- **Sex 4**—Steps to recovering from sexual sin and regret.

Sex as Sweet

When God designed human sexuality, he didn't say it was vulgar and dirty; he said it was good. When God designed the sexual act, he didn't say it was for fun and games by "consenting adults"; he said it was for a committed man and a woman in marriage.

The world says sex is seductive. God says sex is sweet.

The world says sex is for sensuality. The Bible says sex is for expressing deep bonds of love.

SURVEYING THE SESSION

This session helps young adults look beyond society's views of sexuality to recall what God originally intended sex to be. Young adults will:
- make collages to symbolize society's view of sexuality;
- study Bible passages that explore God's views of sexuality; and
- write a letter to God about their attitudes toward sex.

UNDERSTANDING THE WORD

Scripture focus—Genesis 1:27-31; 2:15-25; and 24:67; Song of Songs 1:2-4; 2:3-17; and 4:10; Proverbs 5:18-19; and Hebrews 13:4.

The passages for this session are filled with examples of how God intended sex to be. Beginning where God created humans "in the image of God ... male and female" and continuing in the love songs of the Song of Songs, the wisdom of Proverbs and the commands of Hebrews 13:4, scripture shows the beauty of human sexuality as God's gift.

PREPARING TO LEAD

Before the session, study the passages listed in the Understanding the Word section. Then read the entire session outline. Make sure all the activities fit your group, and make any necessary changes.

Gather the materials for the session. You'll need markers (including a red one), newsprint, old magazines and newspapers, construction paper, scissors, glue and tape. For each person you'll need a Bible, a pen or pencil, a copy of the "Sex in the Bible" handout (page 46), paper, an envelope, three or four chocolate "kisses," and three or four 3×5 cards.

STARTING THE SESSION

Arrange chairs in a circle and welcome everyone. To get better acquainted, ask people each to give their name and tell about their first boyfriend or girlfriend in elementary or junior high school by answering these questions:

- **What was his or her name?**
- **How long did you like him or her?**
- **How did you express your "like"?**

As the leader, go first. Keep the sharing light and fun.

When everyone has shared, write the word "sex" in large, red type on newsprint.

Ask:

- **What was your reaction when I boldly wrote "sex"?**

Write all of the responses randomly on the newsprint. Don't criticize any answers.

Say: **When God designed human sexuality, he saw it as a good gift. Yet we often see sexuality as embarrassing or even evil. That's because sex is often misused and corrupted in our world. This series of sessions looks at God's view of sex and how we as Christians can have healthy attitudes about our sexuality.**

Spread old magazines and newspapers in the center of the group. Form three teams by having people count off by each saying one letter from the word "sex," then have S's form one group, E's form another and X's form the third. Give each team a sheet of newsprint.

Explain that each team will create a collage to illustrate society's view of sex. Encourage teams to use pictures, articles, advertisements, headlines—anything that captures the issue. Have construction paper, scissors and glue available for the groups. As they work, encourage team members to think of examples from their experiences that reinforce the images.

Give teams about five minutes to create, then have them each present their collage and insights to the rest of the group.

Display a sheet of newsprint with two columns—one labeled "Society's View" and the other labeled "God's View." As groups present their impressions, write their major points in the first column. If one group has already made a point, simply underline or checkmark that point when the next group repeats it.

When all groups have shared, add to the list any other insights people think of.

 # DIGGING INTO THE WORD

Form groups of three by having everyone get with two other people so their letters in the previous activity spell the word "sex." If you have extra people, make one or two groups smaller or larger. Give each person a pen or pencil, and a copy of the "Sex in the Bible" handout (page 46). Have groups work together on the handout.

After everyone has finished, have people share their insights. Write the main points on the "God's View" newsprint.

Then ask:

● **What are the similarities and differences between the way the world views sex and the way God does?**

● **Why did God design sex?**

● **When you were growing up, when and how did you learn about sex? What misconceptions were you given? What godly views were presented?**

● **How do you think Jesus would explain sex to a child?**

Applying the Word

Give each person a pencil, a piece of paper and an envelope. Say: **Write a letter to God about sexuality. Talk about how he created us and what sexuality means. Praise and thank him for his gift of sexuality. Be honest about your struggles. Conclude by asking God to lead you to see sex from his perspective.**

Then put the letter in the envelope and seal it. Write your name and address on the outside. Be completely honest with yourself, since the letter will be returned to you unopened during the fourth session.

Collect the envelopes. Remind participants that the envelopes will remain unopened until you return them during the fourth session.

 ## Affirming Each Other

Give people each three or four chocolate "kisses," the same number of 3×5 cards and a pencil. Have clear tape available. Ask people each to tape a kiss to each card, then write an affirmation message on each card to someone in the group. The affirmation doesn't have to relate to the session's topic.

When everyone is ready, have them mingle and privately give their kisses and messages to the appropriate people.

 ## Closing the Session

Form a circle and join hands. Close in sentence prayers, encouraging anyone who wants to pray to say a sentence prayer. End the prayer by thanking God for the gifts of sex and sexuality.

SEX IN THE BIBLE

1. Read Genesis 1:27-31 and 2:15-25.

● Would you conclude from these verses that God designed sex? How did he feel about it?

● What was the purpose of human sexuality?

● Can human sexuality be separated from being human?

2. Read Genesis 24:67; Proverbs 5:18-19; and Song of Songs 1:2-4; 2:3-17; and 4:10.

● What would you conclude about sex from these verses?

● Does it seem to you that sex was designed solely for procreation here? Why or why not?

3. Read Hebrews 13:4.

● What *positive* things does this verse say about sex?

Sex as Sin

$\mathbf{A}$s designed by God, sex is sweet.

But when misused, abused or perverted, sex becomes sin.

When misused, sex loses its sweetness and becomes bitter—even poisonous. It becomes destructive, not constructive; deadly, not life-giving; a curse, not a gift.

Unfortunately, sex is often misused in our world. In fact, misuse is often portrayed as appropriate and healthy. Young adults struggle with these questions as they date, get engaged and marry. They need biblical guidance to help them discern how to make positive choices.

SURVEYING THE SESSION

This session explores the sinful side of sex to help young adults make responsible choices. Young adults will:

- participate in an activity that illustrates how sex changes you;
- discuss two case studies of sexual temptation in the Bible;
- discuss areas where sex may or may not be sinful;
- identify areas where they struggle with sexual temptation; and
- support and encourage each other in personal struggles.

UNDERSTANDING THE WORD

Scripture focus—Genesis 39:1-23 and 2 Samuel 11:1—12:13.

The scripture passages for this session are two familiar but vastly different stories of sexual temptation.

The Genesis passage is the story of Joseph being seduced by Potiphar's wife. Joseph didn't fall for her lure, but she responded to his snub by having him thrown in prison. The story not only illustrates the difficulty of resisting temptation, but it also shows that not giving in can have negative consequences— at least in the short term.

In 2 Samuel we read the story of David and Bathsheba, perhaps the most gripping story of falling for sexual temptation in scripture. As king, David used his power to seduce Bathsheba then have her husband killed in battle. Though David thought his plot was safe, the prophet Nathan told a parable that convicted David of his sin.

 # PREPARING TO LEAD

Before the session, study the passages listed in the Understanding the Word section. Then read the entire session outline. Make sure all the activities fit your group, and make any necessary changes.

Gather the materials for the session. You'll need glue, newsprint and masking tape. For each person you'll need a piece of paper, a Bible, a black marker, a pen or pencil, and a copy of "The Lure of Sex" handout (page 52).

 # STARTING THE SESSION

Welcome young adults as they arrive. Remind them of the series topic, and briefly recall conclusions from the first session.

Form pairs. If you have an extra person, join in the activity yourself. Give each pair two pieces of paper and some glue. Have them glue the two papers together, side by side.

After the glue has dried, have partners try to pull the pieces apart without tearing either piece. When everyone has finished trying, form a circle and have people share their results. Then ask:

● **When you stuck the papers together, how did it affect them?**

● Will either piece of paper ever be the same again?

Say: **In the same way that gluing together two pieces of paper changed them forever, so does sex. When two people unite their bodies in sex, they're never the same after that. So if they weren't meant to be together or if they later try to separate themselves, they can never leave that relationship behind. God can forgive and restore and rebuild your life, but some aftereffects of poor sexual choices are inevitable.**

Ask class members to share their insights and, if they're comfortable, their experiences that illustrate this point.

 # DIGGING INTO THE WORD

Say: **The sinful side of sex isn't a new problem. It's been around from the beginning. And people through history have struggled to avoid the traps of sex as sin. Two biblical accounts illustrate how, when misused, sex can tear apart people and relationships.**

Form two groups. One group can be larger than the other. Have one group study the story of Potiphar's wife and Joseph (Genesis 39:1-23). Have the other group focus on the story of David, Bathsheba, Uriah and Nathan (2 Samuel 11:1—12:13).

Have people in each group prepare to recount the story from a different character's perspective in one minute or less. For example, the first group might have someone tell the story from Joseph's perspective, while someone else tells it from Potiphar's wife's perspective. Encourage people to focus on the sexual issues involved in each story. If you have extra people, some people can watch and share ideas.

Have each person share his or her character's story.

Then ask:

● **What common themes did you pick up in the stories?**

● **How did the stories show sex as sin?**

● **What consequences were there when sex was misused?**

● **How was Joseph's situation similar to David's?**

● **How were the results different? Why?**

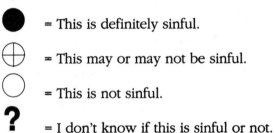

APPLYING THE WORD

Say: **Sometimes it's easy to agree that sex is sinful. But other areas are more controversial and gray. Scripture isn't always clear on the matter, and devout Christians disagree.**

Write the following titles each on a separate sheet of newsprint: Extramarital or Premarital Sex, Homosexuality, Masturbation, Pornography, Watching X-Rated Movies, Sexual Fantasies, Listening to Music With Suggestive Lyrics, Heavy Petting Outside Marriage, and Sexual Attraction. Tape the signs to the room walls. Give people each a black marker, and have them go to each sign and mark it according to their personal beliefs using the following code:

● = This is definitely sinful.

⊕ = This may or may not be sinful.

○ = This is not sinful.

? = I don't know if this is sinful or not.

Allow time for students to mark all the signs. Then briefly discuss each area, focusing on areas of disagreement. Try not to spend much time on each one; just have people raise issues and questions.

Give people each a pen or pencil, and a copy of "The Lure of Sex" handout (page 52). Have them complete the handouts on their own. Urge them to be honest with themselves, since no one else will look at their answers.

When everyone has finished, ask volunteers to share any insights or questions they're comfortable talking about with the group.

Ask:

● **Why are sexual temptations sometimes difficult to resist?**

● **What practical ways have you found that make sexual temptations less tempting for you?**

● **How does God help you overcome temptations**

when you feel them?

● **Knowing we all have sexual desires, how can we avoid sex as sin in our world?**

Write students' ideas on newsprint.

AFFIRMING EACH OTHER

Have young adults form pairs. If you have an extra person, form one trio. Have people each share with their partner one area they'd like their partner to pray for them regarding temptation. Then have partners each pray together, asking God to give their partner strength to resist temptation.

Tell people to keep the prayer concern confidential, and encourage them to touch base with their partners in coming weeks for encouragement and support.

CLOSING THE SESSION

Have the class stand in a circle with eyes closed while you read aloud Psalm 51:10-12—a Psalm attributed to David after Nathan confronted him with his sin.

Then close with a prayer asking God to give each person strength and courage to run from temptation, and to heal the hurts we've inflicted on ourselves and others. Thank God for the power of the Holy Spirit, who enables us to say yes to good and no to evil.

THE LURE OF SEX

For each of the following categories, circle the number that best represents how strongly you feel pulled to get involved in this area of sexuality. Be honest with yourself; no one else will see what you write. If you don't believe a particular issue is sinful, cross it out.

● Becoming involved in premarital or extramarital sex

1   2   3   4   5   6   7   8   9   10

This is no   I can't resist
temptation for me.   this temptation.

● Having a homosexual relationship

1   2   3   4   5   6   7   8   9   10

This is no   I can't resist
temptation for me.   this temptation.

● Masturbating

1   2   3   4   5   6   7   8   9   10

This is no   I can't resist
temptation for me.   this temptation.

● Buying or reading pornographic materials

1   2   3   4   5   6   7   8   9   10

This is no   I can't resist
temptation for me.   this temptation.

● Getting involved in heavy petting outside marriage

1	2	3	4	5	6	7	8	9	10

This is no
temptation for me.

I can't resist
this temptation.

● Watching X-rated movies

1	2	3	4	5	6	7	8	9	10

This is no
temptation for me.

I can't resist
this temptation.

● Having sexual fantasies

1	2	3	4	5	6	7	8	9	10

This is no
temptation for me.

I can't resist
this temptation.

● Listening to music with suggestive lyrics

1	2	3	4	5	6	7	8	9	10

This is no
temptation for me.

I can't resist
this temptation.

● Being sexually attracted to someone other than my spouse

1	2	3	4	5	6	7	8	9	10

This is no
temptation for me.

I can't resist
this temptation.

Two Becoming One

"**M**ost intimate heterosexual relationships have erotic dimensions to them. And it does us no good to deny that fact of life. Rather we should accept these feelings."

Most young adults readily accept these sentences by Richard J. Foster in *Money, Sex and Power: The Challenge of the Disciplined Life* (Harper & Row). Sexual attraction is a natural part of the bonding between men and women.

But it's much harder to respond when Foster writes in the next sentence: "But to accept them does not mean to act upon them."

How can single Christians express their sexuality appropriately? What's the place of romantic attraction and sex in a Christian marriage? What guidelines does scripture give Christians for relating to people of the opposite sex?

This session addresses these questions and appropriate ways for single young adults to express their sexual attraction. And it allows married young adults to examine the role of sex and romance in their marriage.

SURVEYING THE SESSION

This session explores the place of sex in singleness and marriage. Young adults will:
- study Bible passages that offer guidance on sexual relationships;
- identify characteristics of strong relationships that influence sexual relationships;
- develop guidelines for responsible sexual expression; and
- write a love letter to someone they love.

UNDERSTANDING THE WORD

Scripture focus—Song of Songs 3:1-4 and 8:8-10; Matthew 5:27-28; 1 Corinthians 7:3-5, 8-9; and Ephesians 5:22-28.

The passages for this session come from several places in scripture, but they all focus on healthy sexual relationships between men and women.

The two passages from Song of Songs are parts of love songs. The first passage shows a woman yearning for her lover, while the second focuses on controlling sexual passions.

Matthew 5:27-28 contains Jesus' statement that "anyone who looks at a woman lustfully has already committed adultery with her in his heart." Most scholars agree that this passage focuses not on having the fleeting thought, but dwelling on and nurturing it.

The 1 Corinthian passage has two elements. Verses 3 through 5 admonish Christian husbands and wives to respect each other's bodies and needs, and to both be responsible in the sexual relationship. Verses 8 and 9 urge single people to control their passions.

Finally, Ephesians 5:22-28 describes the mutual love between a husband and wife.

PREPARING TO LEAD

Before the session, study the scripture passages listed in the Understanding the Word section. Then read the entire session outline. Make sure all the activities fit your group, and make any necessary changes.

Invite two or three couples who've been married a long time to visit and participate in your class. Explain that you'd like their long-term perspective. Encourage them to participate during the whole session.

Gather the materials for the session. You'll need inflated balloons, a straight pin and several sheets of newsprint. For each person you'll need a Bible, a permanent marker, a heart-shape paper and a pen. (Note: High-quality balloons with "love" imprinted on them are available from Group, Box 481, Loveland, CO 80539.)

 STARTING THE SESSION

As young adults arrive, have them sit in a circle. If you have more than eight to 10 students, form two or more circles. Toss an inflated balloon into the circle, and have young adults keep the balloon in the air.

After a few seconds, toss in another balloon. Keep adding balloons until it's difficult to keep them all afloat. If a balloon hits the ground or goes outside the circle, pop it with a pin. Be sure you keep enough inflated balloons to have one for each class member for the Affirming Each Other section.

After two or three minutes, stop the activity and ask:

● **As I added more balloons, what feelings did you have trying to keep them all inside the circle?**

● **What did you feel when I popped a stray balloon?**

Say: **In some ways, sex is like those balloons. In its proper place in marriage, it's full of life, joy, laughter and promise—just like the balloons in the circle. But if sex leaves its proper place, its joy is replaced by mistrust and pain. And it no longer fulfills its purpose.**

Have young adults reflect more on the analogy. Then introduce the session by saying you'll be focusing on the place of sex in singleness and marriage.

 DIGGING INTO THE WORD

Randomly assign class members each one of the following passages. One person can have more than one verse or several people can have the same verse, depending on your class size. Here are the passages:

● Song of Songs 3:1-4   ● 1 Corinthians 7:3-5
● Song of Songs 8:8-10   ● 1 Corinthians 7:8-9
● Matthew 5:27-28   ● Ephesians 5:22-28

Have people each read their passage and answer these questions:

● **What does this passage say about sex in singleness or marriage? You may have to draw implications from the passage.**

● **What principle regarding sex would you suggest for Christians based on this passage?**

When people have had time to think about their answers, have volunteers read aloud the passages and have people share their conclusions based on the questions. Have other class members add other insights and perspectives.

 ## APPLYING THE WORD

Say: **For Christians, sex is just one part of a many-faceted relationship between a man and a woman. So it's appropriate to think of characteristics of strong relationships as we talk about sex.**

If you have more than eight students, form several groups of no more than eight. Then lay a sheet of newsprint on the floor or on a table in the center of each group. Have several markers available.

On the newsprint, have young adults write—graffiti-style—words or phrases that describe healthy, Christian relationships between men and women who're romantically involved. Examples could include love, shared faith, commitment, respect, intimacy, responsibility, and concern for feelings.

Now have groups talk about how the words and phrases they wrote can influence sexual relationships between a man and a woman—either married or single.

After groups have discussed their sheets, bring them together to share with the whole class. Have the couples you've invited share their insights as well.

Then ask:

● **What role does sex play in marriage? How does it enhance or detract from the marriage relationship?**

● **What are ways sex can be abused in marriage?**

● **How important is romantic love to marriage?**

● **What struggles do married people have with sex? How do they deal with those struggles?**

● **How can single people responsibly satisfy their desire for affection and touch?**

● **What sexual temptations do single people feel? How do they deal with these temptations?**

Divide the class into groups of married or single people. If you don't have one or the other, just have one group.

Ask groups to think of appropriate guidelines for responsible sex depending on whether they're single or married. Encourage them to be as specific as possible, and urge them to focus on positive expressions rather than just a list of don'ts. Have each group list its guidelines on newsprint.

Bring the groups together to report their guidelines. Note and discuss the similarities and differences between the lists.

AFFIRMING EACH OTHER

Give each person a balloon from the Starting the Session section and a permanent marker. Have young adults each write their name on one balloon. Then have them bounce the balloons in the air. When you shout "Stop!" have each person grab a nearby balloon and write an affirmation for the person whose name is on it.

Encourage people to write affirmations about how the person has lived out his or her relationship with members of the opposite sex in a positive way. For example, someone might write, "I always appreciate the affection you show your wife" or "I admire the respect you show for other people."

Bounce the balloons around several times. Then have people each retrieve their own balloon and read the messages.

CLOSING THE SESSION

Give young adults each a heart-shape paper and a pen. Have them each write a short "love letter" to their spouse, boyfriend or girlfriend, or a close friend. Encourage them to express their feelings for that person.

Close with prayer, thanking God for the gift of sex. Ask God to give each person the insight to use the gift as it was intended to be used in relationships.

Encourage young adults each—if they feel comfortable—to give their love letter to the appropriate person.

The Road to Recovery

Our world is filled with people shouting do's and don'ts about sex. Some people say, "If it feels good, do it." Others retort, "If it feels good, it's probably sinful."

Most Christian young adults feel caught in the middle gray area. And when they make mistakes, they're left feeling remorseful and guilt-laden. How can they cope with their feelings, find forgiveness and move on to healthy relationships?

Scripture offers hope. Though Jesus never condoned sin, he always loved the sinner. He was willing to forgive and give a person the opportunity to start over again. And he was always quick to point out that no one is sin-free.

Young adults in your class may be struggling with their own regrets about their sexual involvement. For some, the regrets may be minimal. For others, profound. In both cases, young adults need to hear Jesus say to them: "Has no one condemned you? ... Then neither do I condemn you ... Go now and leave your life of sin."

SURVEYING THE SESSION

This session focuses on recovery, healing and reconciliation from sexual sins. Young adults will:
- discover how sexual sins have lasting consequences;
- discuss Jesus' action in the story of the woman caught in adultery and make modern-day parallels;
- analyze case studies involving recovery from sexual sins;
- reread the letters they wrote to God in the first session; and
- create sand symbols for their feelings about themselves and their sexual choices.

 UNDERSTANDING THE WORD

Scripture focus—John 8:2-11.

Scripture is clear in its condemnation of sexual immorality. Yet condemnation isn't the final word. Forgiveness and healing through Jesus Christ are part of the good news of the gospel.

This passage from John tells about Jesus' response to the woman caught in adultery. Religious leaders brought the woman to Jesus and asked what her punishment should be. The law clearly said she should be stoned, though it had no similar punishment for her sexual partner.

But Jesus challenged the sinless person to cast the first stone. One by one, the leaders walked away, leaving Jesus alone with the woman. He, too, refused to condemn her. He sent her away with instructions to "leave your life of sin."

PREPARING TO LEAD

Before the session, study John 8:2-11. Then read the entire session outline. Make sure all the activities fit your group, and make any necessary changes.

Gather the materials for the session. You'll need newsprint, paper and pencils. For each person you'll need a copy of "The Great Maze" handout (page 64), a marker, a copy of the "Has No One Condemned You?" handout (page 65), a small bag of sand, a piece of paper and the "letters to God" from "Sex 1: Sex as Sweet" session.

STARTING THE SESSION

When everyone has arrived, give each person a copy of "The Great Maze" handout (page 64) and a marker. Have each person use their marker to solve the maze as quickly as possible. Tell them they can never let their marker leave the page. If people make mistakes, just tell them to back up and try again.

When everyone is finished, find out if anyone solved the maze without making any wrong turns. Have others show their mazes—mistakes and all.

Then ask:

● **Why was it difficult to solve the maze without making a mistake?**

● **Did you try to hide your mistakes in the maze? Were you successful?**

● **If you didn't make a mistake, how did you avoid it?**

● **How does solving this maze illustrate the long-term consequences of the mistakes we make in our sexual relationships?**

Say: **In this final session on sex, we're going to look at how we recover from the mistakes we make. As in the maze, we can't erase those mistakes—they'll always be part of who we are. But, with God's help, we can find new hope and healing.**

 # DIGGING INTO THE WORD

Have students close their eyes and try to put themselves in the scene as you read aloud the story of the woman caught in adultery (John 8:1-11). Then form three groups, and assign each group one of the central characters—Jesus, the woman or the religious leaders. Write these questions on newsprint, and have each group answer them from their character's perspective:

● What did you feel at the beginning of the story?

● What are your attitudes toward the other characters in the story?

● What were your feelings when Jesus refused to condemn the woman?

● Was the confrontation settled justly and to your satisfaction?

Have each group report on its discussion.

Then ask:

● **Was the woman the only one who sinned in the story? If not, what other sins were committed?**

● **How were the sinners made conscious of their sin? Explain.**

● **Why was Jesus' final comment to the woman important?**

● **What does this story tell about God's attitude toward people who've been involved in sinful sexual activity?**

● **What modern-day parallels do you see to this story?**

 # APPLYING THE WORD

Form four groups, and distribute the "Has No One Condemned You?" handout (page 65) to each person. Assign each group one of the case studies to discuss and complete. Encourage groups to struggle realistically with the questions instead of offering simple platitudes.

When groups are ready, have them present their conclusions to the rest of the class. Discuss any insights people may have gained from listening to the case studies.

On newsprint, write the following three-step process for seeking forgiveness and restoration:

1. Become aware of sin;
2. Confess sin; and
3. Accept forgiveness, cleansing and recovery.

Have young adults apply the process to the story of the woman caught in adultery. Also encourage them to apply it to contemporary situations they're aware of.

 # AFFIRMING EACH OTHER

Distribute the "letters to God" people wrote during the "Sex 1: Sex as Sweet" session. Ask people each to reread their letters and add any insights they've gained through the study. If any students weren't present for the first study, give them paper, pencils and instructions for writing the letter (see page 45).

Form pairs. If you have an extra person, form a trio. Ask people each to share with their partner one significant thing they've learned from the series and one way their partner can hold them accountable over the next few weeks. Urge people to follow up on the sharing.

CLOSING THE SESSION

Give people each a small bag of sand and a piece of paper. Have them each pour the sand on their paper and use their fingers to sketch a symbol for how they feel about themselves and their sexual choices. For example, someone might shape the sand into two magnets to indicate that he or she always feels pulled in two directions.

Then have people each describe their sand sketch to the group. Encourage people to be honest with their feelings, but respect their privacy if they're reluctant to share.

When everyone has shared, say: **All of us struggle with sin. Even the Apostle Paul constantly battled against his sinful desires.**

Place a large sheet of newsprint in the center of the group. Have people pour their sand onto the sheet in the shape of a cross. As people pour, read aloud Romans 7:15-25.

Close the session with prayer, asking God to forgive and heal each person of the times they've given in to sexual temptation. Ask God to give them the wisdom to "go now and leave their life of sin."

Mail the "letters to God" to students who wrote them in the first session but didn't attend this session, and encourage them to add any insights they've gained in the intervening time.

THE GREAT MAZE

START

END

HAS NO ONE CONDEMNED YOU?

Case Study #1

Andrew only recently became a Christian. Before that, he was active on the "party scene." In fact, his favorite weekend pastime was to pick up a girl on Friday night, spend Saturday and Sunday with her, then dump her. Now Andrew feels regret about his past.

What might Jesus say to Andrew? How can he find recovery, healing and forgiveness?

Case Study #2

Mary and Rod, both Christians, have been dating for two years without getting involved in any heavy petting. Then one evening after final exams during their sophomore year of college, they let themselves go too far and have sex. When Mary's pregnancy test turns out positive, both Mary and Rod are remorseful and confused.

What might Jesus say to Mary and Rod? How can they find recovery, healing and forgiveness?

Case Study #3

Carolyn works in a male-dominated office. She's young, attractive and single, and her colleagues ask her out often. One day her supervisor asks her out. She's been hoping for a promotion, so she decides to take advantage of the situation. But when she gets the promotion and he hints that he gave it to her "as her friend," she feels lousy—like she used another person for her own end.

What would Jesus say to Carolyn? How can she find recovery, healing and forgiveness?

Case Study #4

Tyrone and Martha married right after college graduation. Both became actively involved in their careers. Sometimes they didn't have much time for each other, and they justified the schedule because they "had to get established in their careers."

Now, three years later, they feel like they don't even know each other anymore. They relate more like colleagues than lifelong partners. One day Martha learns that Tyrone has been having an affair. She storms out and goes to live with a relative. Tyrone realizes his mistake, but Martha says it's too late for apologies.

What might Jesus say to Tyrone and Martha? How can they find recovery, healing and forgiveness?

CHRISTIANS AND SUCCESS

How would you measure success? by your annual salary? the size of your house? the number of people who work for you? the titles attached to your name? the honors and awards you've received? the number of friends you have? the type of car you drive? how humorous you are in humorous situations and how powerful you are when the moment calls for power?

Those are some of the standards our culture attaches to success. And many times, the Christian community uses those same standards. A successful church is a church with lots of people, programs, new members and money. Or we "baptize" worldly standards in a "health and wealth" gospel that gives us a "biblical" formula to guarantee worldly success. If you do this or that, then God will bless you with great wealth, good health and everything else you want.

But how does God view success?

The world says, "Get all you can before others rip you off." Jesus says, "Do to others as you would have them do to you" (Luke 6:31).

The world says to look out for #1. Jesus responds, "Whoever finds his life will lose it, and whoever loses his life for my sake will find it" (Matthew 10:39).

How can Christian young adults live what seems like a schizophrenic existence with one foot in the world as they seek to do well at work and one foot in the kingdom of God as they seek to serve Christ? How can they understand success from a biblical perspective?

This series will explore these and other questions about Christians and success. To do this, the studies focus on four questions:

- **Success 1**—What is success?
- **Success 2**—What does it mean to be successful in work?
- **Success 3**—How do money and success go together?
- **Success 4**—What does stewardship have to do with success?

What Is Success?

Living in today's world can make us feel schizophrenic. On the one hand, we feel pulled to be productive, climb corporate ladders and accumulate wealth. These things are the secret to our success. On the other hand, we read in scripture that God sees success in serving others, being obedient to his Word and putting him first.

The two views of success seem contradictory, so we struggle with questions. Can we be successful as businesspeople, students, teachers or nurses and stay true to our faith? Do the outward signs of success—money, power, popularity and prestige—contradict the gospel? And what's a responsible definition of success for Christians?

SURVEYING THE SESSION

This session helps young adults explore their views of success. Young adults will:
- depict and analyze characteristics that make people "successful";
- search for characteristics of success in the book of Ecclesiastes;
- agree on key words in a Christian definition of success; and
- affirm each other for modeling Christian characteristics of success.

UNDERSTANDING THE WORD

Scripture focus—The book of Ecclesiastes.
Ecclesiastes is a book of searching. It begins with the

exclamation, "Utterly meaningless! Everything is meaningless" (Ecclesiastes 1:2b). The rest of the book's devoted to the search for wisdom and meaning in life.

In the process of that search, the "preacher" or "teacher" explores the meaning of success. Several key points in the book include:

- Human efforts apart from God are meaningless.
- Human efforts won't bring happiness or success.
- Accumulating things won't bring happiness or success.
- Life is to be enjoyed as a gift from God.
- Trust and obey God.

 ## PREPARING TO LEAD

Before the session, read the book of Ecclesiastes. It has only 12 chapters and reads quickly. Then read the entire session outline. Make sure all the activities fit your group, and make any necessary changes.

Gather the materials for the session. You'll need tape, newsprint, markers and paper. Photocopy and cut apart the "Views of Success" (page 73). For each person you'll need a Bible, a pencil and six 3×5 cards.

 ## STARTING THE SESSION

Before students arrive, tape two sheets of newsprint to the wall so that each is about the same height as an adult. If you have more than 12 to 15 young adults, tape newsprint to four places. Place several markers near each set of newsprint.

Welcome young adults as they arrive. Divide the class into groups of men or women, and have groups each draw a full-size picture of a "successful" person of their gender.

Encourage participants to draw in as many props as possible (such as briefcases, magazines, computers, cars) to symbolize different things, and have them label specific features. If they ask you to define success more precisely, resist the pressure. Have them use whatever criteria they choose.

After about five minutes of creating, have each group explain its picture of success. Ask:

● **What similarities and differences do you see between the pictures?**

● **What contradictions do you see in the images and symbols?**

Form three groups. Give each group paper, a pencil and one part of the "Views of Success" handout (page 73) to discuss. Have groups each read the description, then write the person's definition of success. Then have them discuss the strengths and weaknesses of the character's view.

Have each group read its statement to the whole class. Then ask:

● **Which of these perspectives do you hear—explicitly or implicitly—these days?**

● **Which perspective do you have the most trouble with? Why?**

● **Which one is most comfortable to you? Why?**

Say: **These examples show how elusive success can be—and how much harder it is to define or measure. In these four sessions, we'll look at success from several angles. We'll begin by developing a biblical definition of success.**

If you wish, summarize the ideas in the introduction to the series on page 67.

 DIGGING INTO THE WORD

Mention that the writer of Ecclesiastes struggled with the meaning of life and success. Form six groups. A group can be an individual or pair.

Assign each group two chapters of Ecclesiastes, and give each group paper and a pencil. Have them each answer the following questions in light of their assigned chapters. Write each question on a separate sheet of newsprint. Here are the questions:

● What endeavors did the writer undertake in his effort to find the meaning of life and success?

● What did he decide was *not* part of success?

● What elements did he include that were part of success?

Have groups work quickly. Then regroup and have groups report their findings. List ideas on the appropriate sheets of newsprint. When all the groups have shared, look at the completed lists and ask:

● **What have we learned from Ecclesiastes about success?**

● **How do you feel about this perspective? Are other pieces missing?**

Write additional ideas on the lists.

APPLYING THE WORD

Give people each five 3×5 cards and a pencil. On each card, have them each write one word they'd include in a Christian definition of success. Ask people to spread the words on a table in the center of the group. Stack together any duplications.

Say: **As a group, select from all the cards the 10 words everyone believes should be in the definition. Don't vote on words; rather try to come to a consensus through discussion and sharing.**

Write the final words on newsprint so everyone can see them.

Ask:

● **What words are most difficult for you to apply in your life?**

● **How do these words conflict or agree with society's view of success?**

● **What are the implications of these words for how we live our lives in today's world?**

AFFIRMING EACH OTHER

Form pairs, and give each person a 3×5 card. Say: **One sign of success in our world is a business card. On your 3×5 card, design a business card for your partner that shows how he or she models success as a Christian. Be as**

creative as possible. You can make up a company name to include, put in a business slogan or draw a logo.

When people have designed the cards, have them each share the card with their partner, then with the whole group. Ask people to give the card to their partner as a reminder.

 ## CLOSING THE SESSION

Ask students to keep a success journal during the course. Through the week, have them write any thoughts or questions they have about success. Also have them note times they've enjoyed the greatest success and endured the greatest failure. Encourage them to keep handouts in their journals.

Form a circle and read aloud Philippians 2:1-11. Then close in prayer, asking God to help young adults evaluate priorities and be more like Jesus.

VIEWS OF SUCCESS

Photocopy and cut apart the following case studies.

Boone and Barbara Townsend

The Townsends epitomize success for the "baby boom" generation. They dress with style—he in a conservative, three-piece suit; she in tasteful suits. Money is rarely an obstacle to them. They're fluent in the languages of investments, acquisitions, art treasures and travel. Boone is president of his own investment firm, and Barbara is the top-selling real estate salesperson in her city.

They have three grown children who are also doing well. Their oldest son, Bo, has a master's of business administration from Harvard and is vice-president of his father's firm. Their daughter is on a U.S. senator's staff and has dreams of someday being a senator too. Their youngest son, Brett, is an all-conference running back in the Big Eight.

When you ask them about success, they have a lot to say. How would they define success?

Bobby Joe Nelson

Bobby Joe believes in a health-and-wealth gospel. He knows what people need to do to have God bless them, and he'll gladly tell you what that is. He's pastor of a booming church that, he believes, confirms his beliefs. Dozens of people join each week. The church is building a multimillion-dollar sanctuary. And Bobby Joe is "blessed" with all the amenities of the "good life." He's "new rich," and wears gold chains and flashy clothes.

Bobby Joe sees no conflict between the Bible and the buck. How would he define success?

Norma Jeremiah

Norma is a no-nonsense, conservative Christian who incessantly quotes from the huge, black Bible—which she *always* carries. She's convinced Christians should have nothing to do with "worldly things," such as money, careers, entertainment and comforts of modern life. She and her family are thinking about moving to the mountains of Montana to avoid any taint of worldly success.

Norma avoids worldly success, and she's always poised to condemn it. How would she define success?

Discovering Success in the Workplace

The meaning of work is confusing. For centuries, philosophers have discussed "work" in all its facets, but they've never reached a consensus.

For instance, Thomas Carlyle writes, "A man perfects himself by working. All work, even cotton spinning, is noble. Work alone is noble." But Herman Melville retorts: "They talk of the dignity of work, bosh. The dignity is in the leisure."

As the two quotes illustrate, the *meaning* of work is debated. What determines work *success* generates just as much controversy. Is success determined by salary, position, office location, power, influence, the amount of vacation time or what? Who succeeds in work? Who doesn't?

This session explores the questions of work and success. If you have full-time students in your class, encourage them to think of past work experiences, their career aspirations or how the subject relates to school.

SURVEYING THE SESSION

This session examines what it means to be a successful Christian at work. Young adults will:
- write an ad for what they think would be an ideal job;
- discuss common assumptions about work;
- study biblical principles about work;
- think about their attitudes toward work; and
- share how they use their gifts to glorify God at work.

UNDERSTANDING THE WORD

Scripture focus—Genesis 1:27-28 and 2:2-3; Ecclesiastes 2:4-11; Matthew 5:13-16; Mark 6:3; Ephesians 4:28; Colossians 3:17, 22-25; 1 Thessalonians 4:11 and 5:12; and 2 Thessalonians 3:10-12.

This session examines several different passages that have implications for a Christian perspective on work. Here are some of the principles you'll discover in these verses:

● Work is God-ordained. People had work to do even in paradise.

● God himself works.

● Life should include a balance of work and rest.

● Because of human sinfulness, work doesn't always bring the fulfillment and joy God intends it to bring.

● Jesus has redeemed our work—just as he redeems everything else.

● We honor and give witness to God through our work.

● For Christians, work's to be done as a service to Christ.

● Hard work deserves honor. Work's important.

PREPARING TO LEAD

Before the session, study the passages listed in the Understanding the Word section. Then read the entire session outline. Make sure all the activities fit your group, and make any necessary changes.

Gather the materials for the session. You'll need markers, newsprint and a toolbox filled with a variety of tools. Photocopy and cut apart the "Work in the Bible" handout (page 80) so each person has one card.

For each person you'll need a pencil, paper, a copy of the "Nine Notions of Work" handout (page 79), a Bible, a copy of the "Work Attitudes" handout (page 81) and a $20 (or $5) bill.

STARTING THE SESSION

Greet young adults as they arrive. Give each person a pencil and several pieces of paper. Say: **Suppose you were flipping through the Sunday newspaper and came across a classified ad for your ideal job. What would the job be? What responsibilities would it include? What would the hours be? salary? location? benefits? When you have a picture in your mind, write the ad for that job.**

Allow two or three minutes for students to write, then have them each read their ad to the rest of the class.

Then ask:

● **What are some common things we want from work?**

● **What role does a job's status or money play in our wishes?**

● **How are our ideal jobs like or unlike our real jobs?**

● **What do our descriptions tell us about what we expect from a job?**

List these ideas on newsprint.

Have young adults sit in a circle. One by one, read the notions of work from the "Nine Notions of Work" handout (page 79). After each one, have students indicate whether they agree or disagree with the assumptions using the following signs:

● Strongly agree—Hold up both thumbs in the air and wave them.

● Moderately agree—Give a simple "thumbs up" sign.

● Disagree—Give a "thumbs down" sign.

● Strongly disagree—Give two "thumbs down" signs, waving arms dramatically.

After the vote, distribute the "Nine Notions of Work" handout and a pencil to each person. Form three groups, and have each group discuss three different notions. Write these questions on newsprint to guide the discussion:

● Have you experienced this notion in your work and relationships? How has it been expressed to you?

● Is this notion widespread in the workplace? in the church?

Allow about 10 minutes for discussion. Then have groups each briefly report on their discussion.

DIGGING INTO THE WORD

Give each student a card from the "Work in the Bible" handout (page 80). Several students can have the same card, but be sure at least one student has each card. If you have fewer than eight people, give some students two or more cards.

Ask students each to read their verses and draw from them a principle of work. Then have them each think about the implications of that principle for their own job.

After two or three minutes, have class members each read aloud their passage and report what they learned. If several people have the same card, compare their thoughts. Then have everyone brainstorm biblical principles of work. List the principles on newsprint.

Conclude the discussion by asking: In light of what you've learned, what does it mean to be a success in work from God's perspective?

APPLYING THE WORD

Give each student a pencil and a copy of the "Work Attitudes" handout (page 81) to complete alone. When people have finished, bring the group together and ask volunteers to share insights and questions.

AFFIRMING EACH OTHER

Put a full toolbox in the center of the group. Ask people each to choose a tool that symbolizes a gift they use in their work to glorify God. Two people may choose the same tool. For example, someone might pick a piece of sandpaper and say, "I try to make work go smoothly for all my colleagues." Ask each person to share. Then encourage other class members to affirm the tools people choose—or to mention another appropriate tool.

CLOSING THE SESSION

Use the closing to introduce the next session, which is closely related to this one. It's about money. Read aloud the parable of the talents in Matthew 25:14-30. Then without comment, give each person a $20 bill. If you can't afford $20 per person, reduce the amount to $5.

Say they can invest that money, hoard it or do whatever they choose with it. The only rule is that they must return $20 (or $5) at the beginning of the next session. Any money they've earned from their investments will be collected and the group will determine what to do with it.

Close the session with prayer. Encourage each person to keep a work journal this week, focusing on their attitudes toward work and success.

NINE NOTIONS OF WORK

In his book *When I Relax, I Feel Guilty* (David C. Cook), Tim Hansel identifies what he calls "nine notions of work" that are common in our society. They are:

1. Work is the primary source of your identity.

2. Work is inherently good, and therefore, the more you do, the better person you are.

3. You are not really serving the Lord unless you consistently push to the point of fatigue.

4. The more you work, the more God loves you.

5. If you work hard enough 50 weeks a year, then you "deserve" a two-week vacation.

6. The purpose of work is to make enough money to buy things so you can be happy.

7. Most of your problems would be solved if you would only work harder.

8. The Bible says that the most important thing a person can do is work.

9. The biggest problem in our society is that people don't work hard enough.

WORK IN THE BIBLE

Cut apart this handout along the dotted lines to make one card for each student.

Genesis 1:27-28 and 2:2-3

Work Principle:

Implications for My Work:

Ephesians 4:28

Work Principle:

Implications for My Work:

Ecclesiastes 2:4-11

Work Principle:

Implications for My Work:

Colossians 3:17, 22-25

Work Principle:

Implications for My Work:

Matthew 5:13-16

Work Principle:

Implications for My Work:

1 Thessalonians 4:11 and 5:12

Work Principle:

Implications for My Work:

Mark 6:3

Work Principle:

Implications for My Work:

2 Thessalonians 3:10-12

Work Principle:

Implications for My Work:

WORK ATTITUDES

Complete this survey as honestly as possible. If you're not currently working, think of past experiences or your school experience.

1. What attitudes do you show others that reflect your attitudes about work? (Check all that apply.)

☐ Enthusiasm   ☐ Sensitivity   ☐ Frustration

☐ Irritability   ☐ Flexibility   ☐ "Look out for #1"

☐ Care for excellence   ☐ Hard work   ☐ Fairness

☐ Honesty   ☐ Sloppiness   ☐ Encouragement

☐ Selfishness   ☐ Boredom   ☐ _____

2. Circle the above attitudes that enhance your Christian witness. Cross out ones that don't. How could you change those attitudes?

3. When you're honest with yourself, which of the below items are most important to you in a job? (Check only three.)

☐ Money   ☐ Using my gifts   ☐ Improving my skills

☐ Helping others   ☐ Power   ☐ Recognition

☐ Colleague relations   ☐ Benefits   ☐ Flexible hours

☐ Work environment   ☐ Prestige   ☐ Following God's call

☐ Office location   ☐ Climbing the ladder   ☐ _____

4. How would you define success in your present job?

5. Would that success enhance or detract from your Christian witness? Explain.

The Meaning of Money

Money—simple metal coins and pieces of paper—makes our world's economy work. It's a valuable commodity to everyone. We'd starve or freeze to death in our world without money.

But just how important is money for Christians? How much can we gain by accumulating wealth? Is our success tied up in the amount of money we make?

Many believe happiness and success are gauged by how much money someone has. But is that an appropriate view? This session examines that question.

SURVEYING THE SESSION

This session helps young adults develop a theology of money and wealth. Young adults will:
- report on your investment from the past session;
- discover attitudes and scriptural principles about money through a fast-paced competition; and
- affirm each other for the "treasures in heaven" they see in each other.

UNDERSTANDING THE WORD

Scripture focus—Deuteronomy 8:10-14; Proverbs 11:28; Proverbs 30:8-9; Ecclesiastes 5:10-11; Haggai 2:8; Matthew 6:19-24; Luke 12:13-21; Luke 16:19-31; 1 Corinthians 4:7; 1 Timothy 6:6-10; 1 Timothy 6:17-18; and 1 John 3:16-18.

These verses are a handful of the many verses in scripture that help us discover a biblical view of money. Among the principles included in these verses are:

- Don't trust money in place of the Lord.
- Don't love money.
- Don't make riches your primary goal.
- Money is a gift from God to be shared.
- Don't regard money as your own; it's God's.

 ## PREPARING TO LEAD

Before the session, read the passages listed in the Understanding the Word section. Then read the entire session outline. Make sure all the activities fit your group, and make any necessary changes.

Ask three vocal class members to advocate these ways to spend the earnings on your investment in the Starting the Session section:

- Use it for a group party.
- Have whoever earned the money keep the profits.
- Use it for missions.

Gather materials for the session. You'll need markers, newsprint, 12 pieces of construction paper, a stopwatch and tape. Design a fake check to award the team that wins the Digging Into the Word game. For each person you'll need a Bible, paper, pencil, a copy of the "Heavenly Credit Card Monthly Statement" handout (page 88) and a "Heavenly Credit Card" (page 87).

 ## STARTING THE SESSION

Follow up your investment from the Closing the Session section of "Success 2: Discovering Success in the Workplace" (page 78). Find out what class members have done with the money you gave them. Ask them to give you the $20 (or $5) back plus any money they earned with the investment. Also ask them to report how they earned the extra amount.

When you've retrieved your investment, compute what additional money has been earned and decide as a group what to do with it. Rely on the vocal class members you recruited to advocate different approaches. When the class reaches its decision, explain that the three people were selected in advance to push their agendas. Discuss how the experiment shed light on how people view money.

Ask:

● **What was the most important consideration in the decision?**

● **What option was least comfortable to you?**

● **What do our attitudes about this money tell us about our attitudes toward money in general?**

DIGGING INTO THE WORD

What does the Bible say about money and success? Before they look at their Bibles, ask young adults to brainstorm what they think the Bible says about money. Tape a sheet of newsprint to the wall, and list their thoughts on newsprint.

Then form two teams. Give each team six pieces of construction paper and a marker. Assign each team the following verses:

Team #1	**Team #2**
Deuteronomy 8:10-14	Proverbs 11:28
Proverbs 30:8-9	Ecclesiastes 5:10-11
Haggai 2:8	Matthew 6:19-24
Luke 12:13-21	Luke 16:19-31
1 Corinthians 4:7	1 Timothy 6:6-10
1 Timothy 6:17-18	1 John 3:16-18

Have teams each write each scripture reference on one side of separate pieces of construction paper. Then have team members work together to decide on the passage's theme regarding money. Have them write each scripture's theme on the back of its paper. Be sure they don't let the other team see or hear what they're writing. When teams are ready, collect the papers and keep them separated by team.

Then say: **We're going to have a competition to see which team can guess what themes the other team found in the passages. When I hold up the scripture reference from the other team, you must work together to agree on the theme. It doesn't have to be worded exactly the same, but it does have to be similar. As soon as you guess one, I'll**

hold up the next reference. The team that guesses the themes fastest wins.

Then add excitement by saying: **This isn't just any race. There's $1,000 at stake. When the clock starts, your team has $1,000. But the amount will decrease by $10 every second. If you guess wrong, we'll cut another $20 off your total. And if the other team finishes in a shorter time, you won't get any money.**

Make sure teams understand. Begin with one team, and ask two people from the other team to help—one to keep time on a stopwatch and another to count the number of incorrect guesses. Have the contest, then total scores. With great pomp, give a fake check to the winning team.

Then ask:

● **How did the prize money affect your guessing?**

● **How did you feel as the prize money slipped away?**

● **What similarities do you see between the game and how we view money in our day-to-day lives?**

Tape the papers with Bible principles beside the newsprint list the group brainstormed at the beginning of the activity. Revise the newsprint list by adding new items that arose in the Bible study, crossing out incorrect impressions and circling ideas on the original list that also appeared in scripture.

Then form pairs. Give pairs paper and pencils, and ask them each to write one or two sentences that summarize a Christian attitude toward money. Have each pair read its statement aloud to the whole group.

 ## APPLYING THE WORD

Ask people to take out their wallets or purses. If some people don't have either, have them list all the things they'd normally have in their wallet or purse. Tell people each to choose one item in the purse or wallet that represents how they apply—or could apply—the biblical principles to their views and use of money. For example, someone could choose a credit card to talk about the temptation to overspend limits. Or someone could choose a picture of a child to show the priority of caring for family.

After everyone has shared, ask:

● **What connections do you see between success and a biblical view of money?**

● **Which is more important: the amount of money you have or your stewardship of your money? Explain.**

Then ask people to find a new partner to discuss these questions:

● **Which biblical principle about money have you had the most success in applying in your own life?**

● **Which principle is most difficult for you to apply?**

AFFIRMING EACH OTHER

Have someone read aloud Matthew 6:19-24. Say: **Often we look at this passage because of what it says about earthly treasures. But it also says a lot about heavenly treasures. And we've all done things that relate to those treasures.**

Give each person a pencil and a copy of the "Heavenly Credit Card Monthly Statement" (page 88). Have them each fill in their name at the top of their statement. Then ask them to pass their statements around the circle. Have each person write on everyone else's statement one "heavenly treasure" that person has added to his or her "account" in the past month (see sample on statement). When the statements return to their owners, allow time for people to read them.

CLOSING THE SESSION

To close the session and to prepare for the next session, give each person a "Heavenly Credit Card" (page 87). Have people each sign the front and list three or four of their personal strengths, talents or gifts around the margins. Then ask people to carry the card with them through the week. Have them jot on the back what they've been doing with those talents.

Close the session with prayer, asking God to give people discernment of how he would have them earn, spend and give their money.

HEAVENLY CREDIT CARD

Photocopy and cut out a card for each student.

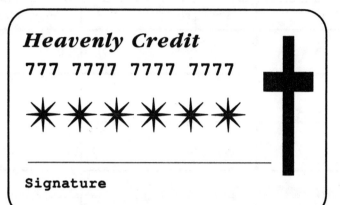

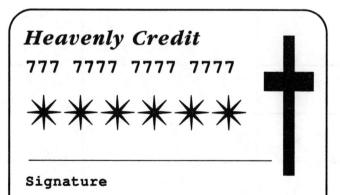

HEAVENLY CREDIT CARD
MONTHLY STATEMENT

Name: _____

Day	Purchase	Amount Due

The Responsibility of Stewardship

The past two sessions revolved around items the world system equates with success: work and money. In this final session, we shift to a more distinctly Christian concept that relates to success: stewardship of time, talents and money.

Jesus calls his people to be good stewards. If Christian success is a close relationship with Jesus Christ and obedience to him, stewardship is a helpful gauge of our "success" as Christians.

Often when we hear the word stewardship, we immediately think of money. But stewardship's much more vast than that. It relates to how we use our time, talents *and* money.

By looking at the parable of the talents in Matthew, young adults will discover principles of biblical stewardship that relate to contemporary issues.

SURVEYING THE SESSION

This session examines our stewardship of money, time and talents. Young adults will:
- answer questions that help them discover their personal priorities regarding time, talents and money;
- study the parable of the talents to discover biblical principles of stewardship of time, talents and money;
- examine their personal stewardship in light of the biblical principles;
- affirm each other for modeling healthy Christian stewardship; and
- commit to improving a specific area of stewardship.

UNDERSTANDING THE WORD

Scripture focus—Matthew 25:14-30.

At its heart, the parable of the talents is about the kingdom of heaven. The unusual story tells how God expects people to use wisely the gifts he's given them.

The story is a familiar one: A man goes on a trip and entrusts his servants with various amounts of money. When he returns, he asks for an accounting. The one who was given the most reports on his great return on his investment. The second servant made a reasonable return on his investment. But the final servant, who was given the least, hid his money and made no return on it. The first and second servants are lauded as "good and faithful servants," while the third is called a "wicked, lazy servant."

While the parable uses money to make its point, it applies to all the gifts God entrusts us with—time, talents and money. Thus it serves as a valuable text for exploring Christian stewardship today.

PREPARING TO LEAD

Before the session, study Matthew 25:14-30. Then read the entire session outline. Make sure all the activities fit your group, and make any necessary changes.

Make a copy of the "Stewardship Stumper Questions" cards (page 94), and cut apart the questions to make cards. Keep the cards in stacks according to category.

Gather the materials for the session. You'll need music (preferably an upbeat song about money) and something to play it on, newsprint, a marker, and an offering plate or box.

For each person you'll need a nickel, dime or quarter, paper, a pencil, a Bible, a copy of "The Buck Stops Here" handout (page 95), four or five pennies, and a piece of play money or a 3×5 card.

 # STARTING THE SESSION

When everyone has arrived, randomly give people each a nickel, dime or quarter. Try to have an even number of people with each denomination.

Play Musical Coins by having young adults stand in a circle and pass their coins one at a time clockwise around the circle while you play the music you selected. After a few seconds, stop the music. If you don't have music, periodically shout "Stop" instead. Have people form groups according to the coin they have. Thus, all nickels form one group; all dimes another; and all quarters another.

Place each category of "Stewardship Stumper Questions" cards (page 94) in a separate area of the room. Label the stacks appropriately. Ask groups each to gather around the stacks as follows:

- nickels around the "Time" stack;
- dimes around the "Talent" stack; and
- quarters around the "Money" stack.

Have each group turn over a "Stewardship Stumper Questions" card, and have each person in each group answer the question.

When each group has answered one question, form a large circle and play Musical Coins again. Have people form new groups according to the same formula and answer a question. Repeat the process a total of four times. Have people stay in their final group for the Digging Into the Word section.

 # DIGGING INTO THE WORD

Explain that this session looks at success in terms of Christian stewardship of finances, time and talents. Stewardship is a key measure of our priorities—or our "success"—as Christians. Add any of your own thoughts or thoughts from the introduction to this session.

Using the same three groups for the last question in the Starting the Session section, assign one group money, one group time and one group talents. Give people each paper and a pencil. Have all three groups study Matthew 25:14-30 and discuss the parable in light of their area of stewardship. The talents group would apply the passage to talents; the money group to money; and the time group to time. Write these questions on newsprint to guide the discussion:

● What does this passage tell Christians about stewardship in your area?

● What's most difficult about this passage as it relates to your area?

● What three stewardship principles for daily living would you draw from this passage?

Regroup and ask someone from each group to report the findings. List all the principles they thought of on newsprint.

Then ask:

● **What new insights did you gain from studying this passage?**

● **What about the passage troubles you the most?**

● **What does this passage tell us about the relationship between stewardship and success?**

APPLYING THE WORD

Distribute a pencil and "The Buck Stops Here" handout (page 95) to each person to complete alone. When group members are ready, have them form pairs or trios to share insights or questions.

AFFIRMING EACH OTHER

Give each person four or five pennies. Say: **Sometimes it's hard for us to evaluate our own stewardship. Often, we're hardest on ourselves. Like the servant in the parable, we sometimes need to hear "Well done, good and faithful servant."**

Have people think of ways they've seen others in the group be good stewards of their time, talents or money. Ask them to privately give people a penny while telling them how they've been models of "good and faithful servants." For example, someone might say, "Don, I really admire the way you've learned to say no to some commitments so you can spend time with your family." As leader, assess who's not getting coins and give some to those people.

Give people several minutes to mingle and exchange pennies. Then encourage people to share pennies with other people in the church as an affirmation of their own stewardship.

 # CLOSING THE SESSION

Give people each a pencil, and a piece of play money or a 3×5 card. Have people write on the money one commitment they want to make to improve their stewardship. It can involve time, talents or money. Encourage them to be honest, since no one else will read what they write.

When everyone's ready, pass around an offering plate or box for people each to place their money or card in to symbolize giving those commitments to God. Join hands in prayer, asking God to give people each the courage and perseverance to follow through on their commitment so he can say to them, "Well done, good and faithful servant!"

STEWARDSHIP STUMPER QUESTIONS

Time	**Talent**	**Money**
1. If you had to choose between helping someone in need and getting adequate sleep, which would you choose? Why?	**1.** If you could develop any talent, what would it be? Why?	**1.** How much money does it take to be happy? Why?

Time	**Talent**	**Money**
2. In what area of life do you feel you spend too much time? Why?	**2.** What's one talent you have that few, if any, people know about?	**2.** If you were given $1 million, how much would you give to the church? Explain.

Time	**Talent**	**Money**
3. If you had only six months to live, what would you do? Why?	**3.** If you had a great talent that required use of your hands then you lost a hand in an accident, what would you do?	**3.** If you could earn twice as much money in a job you thought was unethical, would you do it? Why or why not?

Time	**Talent**	**Money**
4. If you were offered a major promotion, but it would take away from your family and church time, would you take it? Why or why not?	**4.** What person do you admire the most for the way he or she uses his or her talents? Why?	**4.** Which is hardest to be as a Christian— very rich or very poor? Why?

THE BUCK STOPS HERE

Answer the following questions about your stewardship of time, talents and money. Be honest with yourself. You won't have to share anything with other people unless you feel comfortable doing it.

1. Excluding money, what's the most difficult thing for you to give to God? to others? Why?

2. How faithful are you in financially supporting God's work?

3. In what one area—time, talents, money—do you believe God wants you to be a better steward? Why? How can you improve?

4. What connections do you see between stewardship and success in your life?

DISCIPLESHIP AND GOD'S WILL

Last words are lasting words. And Jesus' last words to his disciples concerned God's will for them: "You will be my witnesses in Jerusalem, and in all Judea and Samaria, and to the ends of the earth." (Acts 1:8).

What an awesome responsibility Jesus left to his friends and followers! We Christians today wouldn't be who we are if it weren't for the early disciples' belief, perseverance and willingness to share their lives.

Discipleship was the issue for the first Christians. Obedience was the key to discipleship. And Christ's constant presence was the source for the early church's success.

What does it mean to be a disciple in today's changing world? How do today's young adults follow Christ in their daily lives and choices? How do young adults know what God would have them do as they make plans and struggle with questions about their work, family and future?

This four-session series explores what it means to be a disciple and to follow God's will. These sessions focus on these issues:

● **Discipleship 1**—The ways young adults' faith changes as they grow and mature as disciples;

● **Discipleship 2**—God's will for all his people;

● **Discipleship 3**—Specific guidance for finding God's will when making decisions; and

● **Discipleship 4**—How to keep following Christ, even when it may be unpopular or difficult.

Faith in Transition

Some fundamentals never change.

Keeping your eye on the ball is an enduring truth whether you're hitting a baseball, catching a pass or making contact with a golf club. Properly using dental floss helps prevent tooth decay and gum infection.

The fundamentals of following Christ are enduring as well. Get to know him. Listen to what he says in his Word. And be obedient to what you know to do.

But we change as we grow, mature and have new experiences. Those changes affect our lives and beliefs as Christians. It's one thing to be a believer in high school. It's another to live our faith as a young adult. Our faith needs to change and mature as we ourselves change and mature.

How has our faith changed? What does it mean to be a disciple as an adult? These questions are the focus of this session.

SURVEYING THE SESSION

This session explores the ways faith changes as young adults grow and mature. Young adults will:

- participate in a game that illustrates the complexity of change;
- illustrate Paul's "faith journey";
- draw and explain their own "faith journey";
- affirm their faith in the midst of change; and
- commit to grow in faith in a specific area.

UNDERSTANDING THE WORD

Scripture focus—Acts 9:1-19.

Saul faced many experiences in his life that required him to adjust and grow. As a devout Jew and leader of the persecution of Christians, Saul's perspective was sensationally altered by God's action in his life.

Then as a missionary, Paul experienced both joys and frustrations. By looking at his life, we discover his joy and confidence in preaching the good news. But we also read about his "thorn in the flesh" and his persecution.

Life as a Christian wasn't a constant mountaintop experience for Paul. And that's reassuring to young adults who're experiencing changes and questions about faith as they enter adulthood.

PREPARING TO LEAD

Before the session, study Acts 9:1-19. Then read the entire session outline. Make sure all the activities fit your group, and make any necessary changes.

Gather the materials for the session. You'll need several sheets of newsprint and several markers. For each person you'll need a Bible, paper, a pencil, a dried bean or other seed, and a 3×5 card.

STARTING THE SESSION

When everyone has arrived, do the Knots community-builder. If you have more than 10 people, form groups of six to eight for the activity. Try to have an even number of people in each group.

Have people stand in a circle facing inward. Have them each put their right hand into the center and grab someone else's right hand—but not the person's next to them. Then have people each place their left hand in the center and grab some-one's left hand (not the person next to them), thus forming a knot.

Without letting go of anyone's hand, have people see how quickly they can untie the knot to form a circle again. Sometimes the result will be two intersecting circles.

When the group's finished, ask:

● **What thoughts went through your mind as you formed the knot?**

● **Did you think you'd ever get untangled? Why or why not?**

If a group didn't untangle, discuss the reasons.

● **How was the knot like some of the changes you experience as a young adult?**

● **Which part of the exercise is most like your faith? getting into the knot? being in the middle of the mess? solving the puzzle?**

Say: **In a lot of ways, this knot illustrates changes that take place in our faith. Those changes can be complex and perplexing. And we come out of those changes in a different place than where we started.**

 # DIGGING INTO THE WORD

Have class members brainstorm a list of events they remember from the life of the Apostle Paul. Encourage them to page through Acts to find ideas. List their ideas on newsprint.

Form groups of three or four. Give each group a sheet of newsprint and several markers. Then have each group use the newsprint and markers to create a "Faith Journey Map" for Paul. Have them use symbols to indicate the various obstacles, victories, and ups and downs in Paul's faith journey.

For example, they might draw a big dip or valley to indicate times of frustration; a road with circles to indicate times of confusion; or a wide, climbing road to show times of growth and victory.

As groups begin working, list the following passages on newsprint as guides to some ups and downs in Paul's life:

- Acts 8:2-3
- Acts 9:1-19
- Acts 9:23-25
- Acts 14:19
- Acts 16:22-40
- Acts 27:13-26

- Acts 28:30-31
- 1 Corinthians 15:9-11
- 2 Corinthians 1:8-11
- 2 Corinthians 2:1-4
- 2 Corinthians 11:21b-29
- 2 Corinthians 12:7-10

When groups are ready, have them each explain their map. Then ask:

- **What surprises do you see? What do they mean?**
- **What's missing from these maps?**
- **What changes happened in Paul's faith through the years?**
- **Do you think Paul ever felt confused about his faith? Why or why not?**
- **What comfort do you gain from the ups and downs in Paul's faith journey?**

 ## APPLYING THE WORD

Now give each person a piece of paper and a pencil. Have people each create their own "Faith Journey Map" similar to the one they made for Paul. Encourage them to include times of struggle and security. Have them mark significant events or people who influenced their journey—positively and negatively—along the way.

When people are ready, ask them to share the key points in their faith journeys. Encourage people to share honestly. Don't criticize or challenge anyone about their doubts and struggles.

When everyone has shared, ask:

- **What has changed in your faith and your relationship to Christ in the past five to 10 years? What has caused those changes?**
- **If you'd met Christ on the road to Damascus five years ago, how would he have finished this sentence: "I am Jesus whom you ... "? Why?**
- **What would he say to you today? Why?**
- **How do you see your faith being stretched right now? How can you encourage and support that growth?**

How can we support each other?

Give people each a piece of paper and a pencil. On one side, have young adults write what discipleship meant to them when they were in high school. Then on the other side, have them write what discipleship means to them now. Encourage volunteers to share with the whole group what they wrote.

 ## AFFIRMING EACH OTHER

Say: **Sometimes we feel like our faith is weak—particularly in the midst of changes and questions. Yet even in the midst of change, God assures us of his never-changing love. Our ups and downs don't alter that.**

Read aloud Matthew 17:14-21. Give each person a dried bean or another kind of seed. Say: **This seed is much larger than a mustard seed. But it can remind us that in the midst of change a little faith can sustain us and help us grow.**

Have young adults share with the group ways others in the group help nurture their seeds of faith. For example, someone might say, "Mary, you nourish my faith by always taking time to listen to me when I'm not sure what I think."

Tell young adults to keep the seed as a reminder of how their faith grows even when they have questions.

 ## CLOSING THE SESSION

Give each person a 3×5 card and a pencil. Ask people each to write on the card one area where they believe God is stretching them to grow in their faith. Underneath, have them write steps they'll take to grow in this area.

Encourage volunteers each to share their area and how they'll try to grow. Have people affirm and offer to support each other. Then have people each take their card home as a reminder of their commitment and post it in a place where they'll see it often.

Also ask group members to keep a discipleship journal of what they're learning about discipleship and how God's leading them through the next four weeks.

What Does God Want From Me?

Some people believe discovering God's will is a giant mystery you spend your whole life trying to unravel. Others think God's will is incredibly simple. "Love God and do as you please," they proclaim.

Somewhere between those two extremes is the truth.

The question of God's will is a great concern for Christian young adults. Those in college are making decisions that will affect who they are and who they will become. Other young adults are involved in work and family issues that elicit the question of what God would have them do.

This study helps young adults see that God's will isn't a complete mystery. Through scripture, God has told us many things he would have us do. In this session, young adults will examine scripture to discover God's will for all his people.

SURVEYING THE SESSION

This session explores God's will for all his people. Young adults will:

- express their perceptions of God's will;
- study scripture passages that discuss God's will for all people;
- illustrate where they feel they are in following God's will; and
- affirm each other through a trust-building exercise.

UNDERSTANDING THE WORD

Scripture focus—Micah 6:6-8; Matthew 22:34-40; Romans 12:1-21; and 1 Thessalonians 5:12-22.

In many ways, the entire Bible is an account of God's will for his people. This session focuses on four specific passages that directly address God's will for believers.

The Micah passage directly addresses the question, "What does the Lord require?" It focuses on treating others justly and mercifully and following where God leads.

In the Matthew passage, Jesus captures the essence of the law by challenging people to love God, self and others.

Romans 12 is a more lengthy discourse on Christian living. The passage challenges people to "be transformed by the renewing of your mind." It also reminds us of the differences in the way people appropriately follow God's will. And it concludes by focusing on the importance of love for each other.

Finally in 1 Thessalonians, we read more about the importance of encouraging, supporting and loving fellow Christians. We also are admonished to be joyful, prayerful and thankful in all things, and to hold to good and avoid evil.

PREPARING TO LEAD

Before the session, study the passages listed in the Understanding the Word section. Then read the entire session outline. Make sure all the activities fit your group, and make any necessary changes.

Gather the materials for the session. You'll need construction paper, glue, scissors, crayons, markers, old magazines and newsprint. For each person you'll need a copy of the "Discovering God's Will in Scripture" handout (page 108), a pencil, a Bible and a copy of "The Freeway" handout (page 109).

Starting the Session

Have the construction paper, glue, scissors, crayons, markers and old magazines spread out as young adults arrive. Welcome people and ask them each to use the supplies to create something that symbolizes God's will. For instance, someone might draw a road with different signs along it. Another person might create a collage of various activities. Create something yourself.

When everyone has finished, ask them each to share their creation with the group. To encourage openness, begin the sharing yourself.

Then discuss the different perceptions of God's will. Ask:

● **What do all the different expressions tell us about God's will?**

● **What do the similarities between different expressions tell us?**

● **How did you discover this picture of God's will?**

● **What analogies have you heard to explain God's will? Which ones are helpful to you?**

 # Digging into the Word

Ask the group to brainstorm when people often ask the question, "What's God's will?" List their ideas on newsprint.

Then say: **When we think of God's will, we usually think about big life decisions. But God's will really involves more than big decisions. It involves how we live our lives from day to day. And scripture gives us many answers to the question, "What's God's will?"**

Form four teams. If you have more than 16 people, form teams of three or four and give more than one team each passage. Give each person a copy of the "Discovering God's Will in Scripture" handout (page 108) and a pencil. Assign each team one of the following passages to study in light of the handout:

● Micah 6:6-8   ● Romans 12:1-21

● Matthew 22:34-40   ● 1 Thessalonians 5:12-22

After groups have finished the handout, gather everyone together. Ask groups each to report what they found to be God's will. List their suggestions on newsprint. If different groups found similar points, put checkmarks on the newsprint by the ones that are repeated.

Ask:

● **How do these passages change your perception of God's will?**

● **How can we learn to apply items marked with a question mark?**

 # APPLYING THE WORD

Give people each a pencil and a copy of "The Freeway" handout (page 109) to complete on their own. When everyone's finished, form pairs. If you have an extra person, form one trio. Have pairs each share their illustration.

 # AFFIRMING EACH OTHER

As a group, brainstorm how Christians can help each other stay on the "freeway" of God's will. List ideas on newsprint.

Then stand and form a tight circle. If you have more than 10 people, form smaller circles. Say: **Part of being a community of faith is trusting and supporting each other as we seek to follow God's will.**

To symbolize this mutual accountability and how we guide each other, have one group member stand in the middle of the circle. Have people in the circle hold their palms out in front of their chests.

Then with knees locked and eyes closed, have the person in the middle slowly fall backward toward someone without moving his or her feet. When that person stops the fall, have him or her gently push the person onto the palms of the next person, and so on. Have the center person rotate all the way around the circle without moving his or her feet or bending his or her knees.

As each person in the circle holds up the person in the middle, have the outside person say, "I'm here for you, (name)." Have each person take a turn in the center.

 ## CLOSING THE SESSION

Close by reminding young adults that the secret to following God's will isn't in psyching themselves up to do well. It's in trusting Christ to work through them. Read aloud Philippians 2:12-13.

Have a silent prayer and encourage people to pray for themselves and one another that they might do what they know to do. Close the prayer by asking God to work through people so they may each live according to God's will for his people.

DISCOVERING GOD'S WILL IN SCRIPTURE

1. Read the scripture assigned to your group. Then write everything in the passage that describes God's will for his people.

2. Looking at the list in #1, underline items that seem clear and simple. Circle items that seem unclear. And put a giant question mark beside those that seem impossible to fulfill.

3. In one sentence, how would you summarize God's will based on this passage?

THE FREEWAY

Imagine God's will as a freeway. It has boundaries and is headed in a particular direction. There's room on the freeway for everyone who wants to travel on it. And people can choose how they want to travel. Some may be in the fast lane, while others are in the slow lane. Some may be out front, while others are at the back. Some travel alone, while others travel together.

On the illustration below, draw symbols to show where you fit on "God's freeway." Add any turns, service roads, detours or other elements you think are appropriate. Which lane are you in? How fast are you traveling? Who's with you, if anyone? What signs are you following? Is it daytime or nighttime? What are the road conditions?

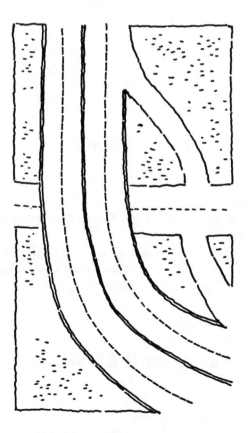

What Now, Lord?

How do you decide what job to take? whether to marry? which option to choose in a dilemma? Do you read tea leaves or horoscopes? look for open and closed doors? panic, but do nothing? pray, and do something?

Following God's will in decision-making sometimes isn't easy. Usually God doesn't send a supernatural sign that leaves no question of what to do. More often, we have to rely on God's Word and the gifts God has given us—discerning minds and supporting friends—as we make choices.

This session explores how we find God's will in specific situations.

SURVEYING THE SESSION

This session gives specific guidance for finding God's will when making decisions. Young adults will:
- experience what it's like not to have clear guidance from others;
- study the story of Gideon seeking a sign from God;
- explore principles for discovering God's will; and
- apply those principles to a personal dilemma.

UNDERSTANDING THE WORD

Scripture focus—Judges 6:17-24, 36-40.

The sixth chapter of Judges tells the story of Israel being taken over by the Midianites. The conquerors destroyed the crops, killed the animals, ravaged the land and left the Israelites frightened and impoverished (Judges 6:2-6).

Hearing the cries of the oppressed Israelites, God called Gideon to "save Israel out of Midian's hand" (Judges 6:14). Gideon was reluctant. He argued that he was the "least" in his family, and his family was the "weakest" clan in the tribe (Judges 6:15).

God hadn't come to the obvious leader, and Gideon was a very reluctant warrior. He repeatedly asked God for a sign— something to confirm what he was supposed to do. His story is an appropriate launch pad for discussing how we discover God's will.

PREPARING TO LEAD

Before the session, study Judges 6:17-24, 36-40. Then read the entire session outline. Make sure all the activities fit your group, and make any necessary changes.

Gather the materials for the session. You'll need newsprint and markers. For every four to six people you'll need a blindfold, a pencil sharpener, a piece of paper and a letter-size envelope. For each person you'll need a Bible, a copy of the "Signs of God's Will" handout (page 115), a pencil, paper and a marker.

STARTING THE SESSION

Form groups of four to six, and give each group a blindfold. Have each group choose one person to blindfold by having one person hold a corner of the blindfold. Then go around the group with each person grabbing the blindfold just below the other person's hand. Have teams blindfold the person who grabs the very bottom of the blindfold.

When someone from each team is blindfolded, write the following instructions on newsprint.

1. Sharpen the pencil.
2. Write something on the paper.
3. Fold the paper and put it in the envelope.
4. Seal the envelope and leave it on the table.

Set a pencil sharpener, pencil, piece of paper and letter-size envelope on a table for each team, and have the teams each lead its blindfolded person to their table.

On "go," have the blindfolded people race against each other to finish the tasks. Teams can coach, but they may only answer questions with "yes" or "no." No one but the blindfolded person can touch any of the supplies.

When all the groups have finished, ask:

● **What was the most difficult part for the blindfolded people?**

● **What was difficult about giving guidance?**

● **Did blindfolded people appreciate the guidance given? Was it clear? How could it have been more helpful?**

● **How was the activity like or unlike receiving guidance from God?**

 # DIGGING INTO THE WORD

Say: **Sometimes trying to learn God's will seems like being blindfolded. We desperately need direction. We wish someone would yank off the blindfold so we could see everything clearly.**

Remind people about the story of Gideon, using the information in the Understanding the Word section. Explain that Gideon was in a similar situation. Even though he had direction from God, he wanted God to give a sign to assure him he was doing the right thing. Then read aloud Judges 6:17-24, 36-40.

Have people rejoin their groups from the Starting the Session section. Ask the following questions, giving groups time to discuss each one after you ask it:

● **Why do you think Gideon wanted to put God to a test when verse 36 indicates that God had already promised Gideon success?**

● **Do you think Gideon tested God because he didn't trust him or because he was afraid of failing?**

● **Why did Gideon ask God not to be angry with him? Do you think God becomes angry when we seek direction?**

● **Do we sometimes overdo it when asking God for signs? How obligated is God to answer these requests?**

Conclude the discussion by asking anyone who has had a

sign from God to share that experience. Also ask if anyone thought he or she had a sign from God only to decide later that it probably wasn't a sign. Talk about how either event affected that person's faith and trust in God.

 ## APPLYING THE WORD

Say: **Sometimes we wait for God to give us a miraculous sign of his will when he has already given us his Word, our minds and each other to help us make good decisions.**

Form four new groups. Give each person a copy of the "Signs of God's Will" handout (page 115), a pencil and paper to keep notes. Assign each group one of the principles. Have groups each read their case study and discuss its principle. Then have people think of situations they've experienced when they used—or could've used—that principle in seeking God's will.

When groups are ready, have them each report their principle to the whole group.

Then ask:

● **Which principles are most comfortable for you? most difficult?**

● **Do any of the principles seem to be in conflict with each other? If so, which ones?**

● **What other principles have you found for discovering God's will?**

 ## AFFIRMING EACH OTHER

Give each person a piece of paper and a pencil. Ask people each to write one decision they're trying to make right now regarding God's will.

Form pairs. If you have an extra person, form one trio. Have people each share with their partner the decisions they're struggling with. Using the principles from the handout, have partners talk through which principles can help with each decision. Encourage partners to pray for each other in making their decisions.

CLOSING THE SESSION

Put a large sheet of newsprint on a table, and have the group sit or stand around it. Give each person a marker. Remind people of how Gideon asked for a sign from God.

Then say: **Like Gideon, we all wish for signs to make our choices easy. But that's not how God usually reveals his will. At the same time, God has given us signs—signs that he'll guide us. Those signs are the times when God has guided us in the past.**

Have people think of times they've looked back on an experience and have seen God's hand guiding them. Ask them to write those memories on the newsprint in shapes of appropriate traffic signs, such as stop signs, yield signs and caution signs.

When everyone has written, close with prayer and thank God for the guidance he gives.

SIGNS OF GOD'S WILL

Read the case study assigned to your group. Then discuss your principle. Talk about times you've used—or could've used—this principle in seeking God's will.

It was time for Lori to declare her college major. She'd been planning on a drama degree since she left high school, but she'd also become interested in teaching English literature. She knew she had skills in both areas, and she knew God could use her equally well in whatever career she chose. So the night before she had to make her decision, she went through a list of pros and cons, pluses and minuses one more time. The next day she made her decision.

Tyrone had been working for a large, international accounting firm ever since he graduated from college six years earlier. He'd climbed the corporate ladder well and made good money. But he yearned for a more entrepreneurial job. Then one day a real estate development firm offered him a job. The salary was a lot less than he was making. But he was fascinated by the creative side of real estate development.

To help make his decision, he called his father—a savvy executive. He also met with a friend in real estate development and an older accountant he respected. Two weeks later he made his decision.

continued

Principle #3: The Revealed Will of God

Peter and Lynn had been dating for more than a year and were engaged to marry in two months. They'd already leased an apartment where they'd live after they married. As the wedding approached and expenses piled up, Peter and Lynn wondered whether it would be best to move in together to save rent.

To help make their decision, they read the Bible together, focusing on passages about love, marriage and sexual conduct. When they finally made their decision, they were convinced it reflected God's will as revealed in scripture.

Principle #4: You Can't Lose

Manuel, a Christian leader, was asked to become pastor of a metropolitan church in another part of the country. He'd been out of the pastoral ministry for several years while he worked in a Christian organization and did some writing. He didn't know if he could still lead a church effectively. And he didn't know whether God wanted him to move.

So he asked eight people—his family and closest friends—to vote on this call. When the results were added up, four people recommended he take the church and four recommended he turn it down.

Manuel complained that the vote didn't provide much direction, but he sensed God saying, "What do you have to lose by going?" If he went and failed, the church would probably survive and he'd be able to write a book about his failures. But if he didn't go, he might miss a wonderful opportunity to do something significant in the kingdom. He couldn't lose.

When the Going Gets Tough

Some people say there's an 80 to 20 rule in life. Eighty percent of life is fighting an uphill battle, and only 20 percent of life is coasting downhill.

Whether the proportion is accurate or not, life certainly isn't a long downhill coast. People all face uphill struggles. And the uphill climb sometimes involves doing what God wants us to do—even when it would be easier to coast downhill in a different direction.

What are the benefits of hanging tough when the world tells us to take it easy? What's the cost of discovering God's will and doing it? This final session in the series on discipleship addresses these questions.

SURVEYING THE SESSION

This session challenges young adults to keep following Christ, even when living their faith may be unpopular or difficult. Young adults will:

- simulate what it's like to be persecuted for their faith;
- study models of faith in scripture;
- discuss case studies of people who've had to make tough choices about the cost of discipleship;
- share faith models who lead them in their discipleship; and
- recall highlights of this series on discipleship.

 UNDERSTANDING THE WORD

Scripture focus—Hebrews 11:32-40.

Hebrews 11 pulls together the entire Old Testament, reminding readers of those who've gone before and modeled faith in God even in the tough times.

This session focuses on the conclusion of the chapter, where the author recalls the judges and prophets. We're reminded of the trials, persecution, torture and even death they faced because of their faith.

The passage is a vivid reminder of the cost of following Christ. Through it young adults can find new courage to stand firm in their faith.

PREPARING TO LEAD

Before the session, study Hebrews 11:32-40. Then read the entire session outline. Make sure all the activities fit your group, and make any necessary changes.

Gather materials for the session. You'll need marshmallows (enough for half of the students each to have a dozen or more), newsprint, markers and tape. For each person you'll need a strip from the "God's Faithful People" handout (page 121), a Bible, a pencil, a copy of "The Cost of Following Christ" handout (page 122) and a 3×5 card.

STARTING THE SESSION

When everyone has arrived, form pairs. If you have an extra person, form a pair with him or her, and be the interviewer. Have pairs decide which person will be the interviewer and the interviewee. Don't explain the activity. Then have all the interviewers go out of the room so you can explain the interview to them.

When interviewers are outside, give each one a dozen or more marshmallows. If you don't have marshmallows, use paper wads. Tell interviewers each to ask their partner questions that will elicit answers that include the following words: "God," "faith," "church," "Jesus," "believe," "Bible" and "Christian." Then when their partner says one of the words, have the interviewers each throw a marshmallow at the person. Urge them not to reveal to the interviewee what's going on.

When everyone understands the activity, have partners do the interviews for one or two minutes. Then bring the group together for discussion.

Ask the interviewees:

● **What thoughts went through your mind when your partner started throwing marshmallows?**

● **When you discovered what words prompted a marshmallow to be thrown, did you change how you answered questions?**

Ask the interviewers:

● **What feelings did you have as you asked questions and threw marshmallows?**

● **Were there times when you didn't throw a marshmallow when you should've? Why didn't you?**

Ask everyone:

● **What parallels do you see between this activity and discipleship?**

 # DIGGING INTO THE WORD

Read aloud Hebrews 11:32-40. Give each person a strip from the "God's Faithful People" handout (page 121). More than one person can have the same strip. If you have fewer than seven people, give people each more than one strip. If several people have the same strip, have them work together. Have people each look up their passage and be ready to report on the price that person paid for his or her faith.

When people are ready, have them report to the group. When all the stories have been told, read aloud Hebrews 11:32-40, which commends the faith of the people class members just studied.

Ask:

● **What's the good news in this passage?**

● **What's the difficult news in this passage?**
● **What could these people teach us about God's will?**

APPLYING THE WORD

Form three groups, and give everyone a pencil and a copy of "The Cost of Following Christ" handout (page 122). Assign each group one of the case studies to read and discuss.

When groups have finished, gather everyone together. Ask each group to read its situation and report briefly on its discussion.

Then ask the whole group:
● **Which of the cases presents the toughest decision for you? Why?**
● **Which costs of discipleship are hardest for you to pay?**

Have the group brainstorm some costs people face today because of their faith. Focus particularly on costs people in the group face. List their ideas on newsprint.

Then ask:
● **When have you had to pay a price because of your faith?**
● **What cost is your faith to you now? Is it worth it to you? Explain.**

AFFIRMING EACH OTHER

Tape a sheet of newsprint to the wall. Draw a cloud on it. Give each person a pencil and a 3×5 card. Remind people of the scripture passage you studied about the heroes of faith. Then read Hebrews 12:1-3, the passage that immediately follows the faith passage.

Say: **Like the writer of Hebrews, we too, are surrounded by "a great cloud of witnesses"—faithful Christians who encourage us as we seek to follow God.**

On their 3×5 card, have people each write the name of someone they look up to as a model of faith and who they admire for accepting the cost of discipleship. Then have people each tape their 3×5 card to the newsprint cloud to symbolize this cloud of witnesses. As they each tape the name to the cloud, have them call out the person's name. It's not important that others know the person who's mentioned.

When people have all added their names, lead in a prayer of thanks for those who model discipleship so others "will not grow weary and lose heart" (Hebrews 12:3).

 ## CLOSING THE SESSION

Conclude this session by thinking back on the whole series with an exercise called "I Learneds." Ask volunteers to share things they've learned through the series. As they do, write these "I learneds" on newsprint.

Close in prayer, asking volunteers to thank God for what's been learned through the series.

GOD'S FAITHFUL PEOPLE

Photocopy and cut apart the following strips. You'll need one strip for each participant.

Gideon—Judges 8:1-21	Deborah—Judges 4:1-24
Samson—Judges 16:4-31	Jephthah—Judges 11:29-39
David—1 Samuel 18:1-29	Samuel—1 Samuel 8:1-22
Jeremiah—Jeremiah 26:1-16	

THE COST OF FOLLOWING CHRIST

Jeff—Jeff became a committed Christian during his sophomore year in college. For more than a year, he has been dating a woman who isn't an active Christian.

In the year since he became an active Christian, Jeff has felt like he should break up. But that thought scares him. He does almost everything with his girlfriend. In fact he hasn't even bothered to keep up other friendships. Who would he talk to? Would his friends support him?

But despite his fears, Jeff truly believes God is calling him to give up his romantic relationship with his girlfriend because their values, priorities and directions are so different.

Discuss in your group:
● What would you say to Jeff?
● What might happen if Jeff doesn't break up? if he does?
● What would you do in this situation? What would worry you the most if you were in Jeff's place?

Tonya—Tonya is a systems analyst in a major computer firm. She has a well-paying position, and her future is bright in the firm. Her boss encourages her by insisting that she'll be promoted to department supervisor before long—which would mean a substantial pay raise.

But there's a tug inside her. She's been asked by a Christian ministry organization to join the staff to develop and operate its computer system. The ministry is one she has always supported and felt drawn to. But the salary would be less than half of what she's making now—and she'd have no opportunities for advancing. What should she do?

Discuss in your group:
● What advice would you give Tonya?
● What could happen to Tonya if she takes the new job? if she stays in her present job?
● How difficult would it be for you to leave a job you really enjoyed and that paid well? What would your friends and family say?

continued

Ryan—When Ryan took his job at the law firm after law school, he was delighted with the position. The firm is prestigious. The pay is great. And the hours are reasonable. He fits in well, and people seem to appreciate his work.

But Ryan struggles with the company's policy on which cases to take. He'd gone to law school so he could help people who'd been treated unjustly or had been discriminated against. But the firm refuses most cases that don't promise to make a lot of money. And it never takes a controversial case—regardless of how important the case might be.

Now Ryan has just learned that the company has turned down a case simply because of the client's ethnic background. As a Christian, Ryan believes he should confront the partners about the blatant injustice. But he also knows he could lose his job for doing so. What should he do?

Discuss in your group:

● What advice would you give Ryan?

● What might happen if Ryan confronts the partners? if he doesn't?

● When, if ever, have you been in a situation similar to Ryan's? What happened?

GROWING IN FAITH

From the time we were toddlers, we've been bombarded by the fact that there are four basic food groups: meat, fruits and vegetables, dairy products and breads. And we must eat from all four to be healthy.

The same holds true for spiritual nourishment. There are also four basic "spiritual food groups" that are necessary for healthy, balanced spiritual development. These four are Bible study, prayer, fellowship and evangelism. If we neglect any one of the four, we deplete our soul of nutrients necessary for good spiritual health.

Each "spiritual food" teaches us something different about God, ourselves and the world. For instance, we read about God's power in the Bible. We connect with God's power through prayer. We hear about God's power in the lives of others through fellowship. And we experience God's power as he changes lives through evangelism.

But no one keeps a perfect balance of all four. That's why this series is called, "Growing in Faith." We gradually move to spiritual maturity just as we do to physical maturity. That maturation process takes time, but we can help the process with practical steps. This series gives practical ways to take those steps. These session focus on the following issues:

● **Spiritual Growth 1**—What enhances and inhibits spiritual growth;

● **Spiritual Growth 2**—How to develop a spiritual life through prayer;

● **Spiritual Growth 3**—How to study the Bible; and

● **Spiritual Growth 4**—The importance of fellowship and evangelism to Christian growth.

Spiritual Gardening

We all take care of ourselves. We eat (sometimes too much). We sleep (not as much as we'd like). We exercise (on good days). And we dress to protect ourselves (even if the clothes are wrinkled).

While we take care of our physical needs, sometimes we neglect our spiritual needs. Somehow we expect to stay in good spiritual health without much work.

But it doesn't work. Just as our muscles grow weak without exercise, so our spiritual life loses strength without use.

This session begins the series on spiritual growth with a different analogy: farming. Using a common image from his day, Jesus tells a story about a farmer's field that says a lot about spiritual growth. He tells about the dangers of not "cultivating" your spiritual life. And he suggests what happens when you do take care of your "spiritual soil."

SURVEYING THE SESSION

This session examines what enhances and inhibits spiritual growth. Young adults will:
- draw parallels between a balanced diet and balanced spiritual growth;
- create dramatic interpretations of the parable of the sower and apply it to contemporary life;
- identify the "soils" in their own lives and different factors that enhance or inhibit their spiritual growth;
- affirm each other for encouraging each other's Christian growth; and
- commit to addressing obstacles they face in spiritual growth.

UNDERSTANDING THE WORD

Scripture focus—Mark 4:1-20.

The parable of the sower might more accurately be called the parable of the soils, since the focus is on how the seeds— God's Word—is received by different soils.

This parable is one of the few in scripture that includes a lengthy explanation. Jesus parallels what happens to the seeds in the field with how people receive his Word. For some people, the Word never sinks in, because "Satan comes and takes away the word that was sown in them" (Mark 4:15).

Others receive the Word with joy, but their faith is shallow and they fall away when under pressure. Still others accept the Word, but other worries, deceits and desires choke out the Word. Finally, those whose lives are prepared to hear the Word, receive it and it grows bountifully.

PREPARING TO LEAD

Before the session, study Mark 4:1-20. Then read the entire session outline. Make sure all the activities fit your group, and make any necessary changes.

Gather the materials for the session. You'll need samples of food from each of the four food groups (meat, fruits and vegetables, dairy products and breads), newsprint and a marker. For each person you'll need a Bible, a pencil, a copy of the "Personal Garden Plot" handout (page 131), paper and a copy of the "Garden Trouble-Shooting" handout (page 132).

STARTING THE SESSION

Before people arrive, arrange the foods you brought from the four basic food groups on a table in the center of your room.

When everyone has arrived, have them sit or stand around

the table. Have young adults identify the four food groups, then ask people each to choose a food from the table that most resembles them—their personality, outlook or other characteristics. More than one person can choose a specific item. Then ask people each to tell why they picked their food. For example, people might choose bread because they aren't fancy, but they provide basic nourishment in their relationships.

Introduce the series on spiritual growth by drawing parallels between the four food groups and the four "spiritual food groups"—Bible study, prayer, fellowship and evangelism. Encourage people to add their own thoughts. Ask people to draw parallels between a balanced diet and balanced spiritual growth.

Then draw two columns on newsprint. Label one "A Balanced Spiritual Diet" and the other "Junk Food." Have the group brainstorm things that help people grow spiritually. List ideas in the first column. Then list things that hinder spiritual growth in the other column.

DIGGING INTO THE WORD

Have someone read aloud Mark 4:1-9. Then form four groups. They don't all have to be the same size. Assign each group one of the soils in the parable—hard soil, rocky soil, thorny soil and good soil. Ask the groups each to develop a 45-second skit, pantomime or other dramatic presentation that depicts their assigned soil and what it symbolizes today.

Allow several minutes for groups to prepare, then have them each present their skit. When the skits are over, have someone read aloud Mark 4:10-20.

Ask:

● **How does Jesus' explanation change your perception of the parable?**

● **What specific message is the sower sowing?**

● **How can we prevent Satan from stealing the Word from people who've recently heard it?**

● **What does it means to have good roots? Give some contemporary examples of people with poor roots—but don't use their names.**

● **What are some worries of the world? How do they**

choke the Word?
● **What happens when the Word becomes fruitful?
How can we tell if a person is good soil and bears fruit?**

APPLYING THE WORD

Give each person a pencil and a copy of the "Personal Garden Plot" handout (page 131).

Ask people to work alone on the handout. Assure them they won't have to share anything from the handout they're not comfortable sharing.

When people have finished, ask if anyone would like to share an insight from the handout.

Then ask:

● **Which area of spiritual growth is easiest for you? Why?**

● **Which is most difficult? Why?**

● **If you could change just one of the soil conditions in your garden in the next month, which one would you change? Why?**

● **If Jesus were the gardener in your spiritual garden, would he be satisfied with the harvest? Why or why not?**

AFFIRMING EACH OTHER

Give each person a pencil and a piece of paper. Have people form pairs with someone they know well. If you have an extra person, you can join this activity.

Say: **While Jesus is the master gardener in our lives, he has given us each other to care for our spiritual well-being. On your piece of paper, draw a garden tool or supply that represents how your partner helps you take care of your spiritual growth. For example, you might draw a hoe to symbolize how the person always challenges you to "dig deeper" into your questions.**

Have anyone who's new or doesn't know his or her partner well talk about someone else in his or her life.

Allow time to draw, then ask people each to share their partner's symbol with the rest of the group.

 ## CLOSING THE SESSION

Give people each a pencil and a copy of the "Garden Trouble-Shooting" handout (page 132) to complete on their own. Allow time to share for any students who wish to share what they wrote, but don't force anyone to share.

Then join hands in a circle to close in prayer.

PERSONAL GARDEN PLOT

The garden plot below has the same conditions as the field in the parable of the sower. Fill in the details in the garden as follows:

● Label the row markers in each soil according to how you feel about your spiritual growth and discipline in that area of your life. For example, if other things tend to crowd out Bible study, you might write Bible study on the row marker in the thorny soil.

● In the tool shed, label some tools you use to keep your "spiritual garden" in good condition. For example, you might label a packet of seeds "listening to sermons."

● In the buckets, indicate how much harvest you expect from your spiritual garden.

● Add other details to the garden that fit your situation.

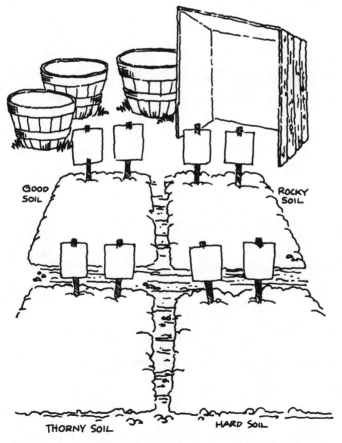

GOOD SOIL

ROCKY SOIL

THORNY SOIL

HARD SOIL

GARDEN TROUBLE-SHOOTING

Think about a specific problem in your spiritual growth. Then complete this handout on your own.

1. Symptoms of plant trouble, such as boredom or lack of commitment:

2. How long it has been a problem:

3. How extensive the problem is:

4. What's wrong—based on the parable:

5. How to get rid of the problem:

6. Specific things you'll do in the next week:

Hotline to Heaven

"Lord, teach us to pray."

That was a disciple's request that prompted Jesus to give his Model Prayer (Luke 11:2-4). They wanted to become people of prayer—just as he was.

Christian young adults today often make the same request. They're aware of the importance and power of prayer. But sometimes they don't feel they know how to do it. Their childhood prayers seem inadequate, and they don't feel they have the experience of other adults in prayer.

By learning to pray, we'll add a vital "meal" to our "spiritual diet." This session looks at the elements of prayer and gives young adults a chance to practice praying.

SURVEYING THE SESSION

This session gives practical handles for developing a spiritual life by understanding and learning to pray. Young adults will:

- brainstorm prayer hang-ups—excuses for not praying;
- look at four elements of prayer;
- practice different forms of prayer;
- remember the importance of praying for each other; and
- be encouraged to keep a personal prayer journal.

 UNDERSTANDING THE WORD

Scripture focus—Psalm 33:1-5; Matthew 7:7-12; 1 Thessalonians 5:18; Hebrews 4:15-16; and 1 John 1:8-10.

The scripture passages for this session each deal with one

of the four elements of prayer: adoration, confession, thanksgiving and petition.

Psalm 33 is a Psalm of praise and adoration to God. It illustrates the joy and variety we can bring to our prayer of adoration. The Matthew 7 and Hebrews 4 passages remind us that God hears our prayers of petition in which we ask God to grant our requests. 1 Thessalonians 5:18 calls Christians to thank God in all circumstances. And the 1 John passage invites us to confess our sins to God, knowing he'll forgive us.

 # PREPARING TO LEAD

Before the session, read the passages listed in the Understanding the Word section. Then read the entire session outline. Make sure all the activities fit your group, and make any necessary changes.

Gather materials for the session. You'll need newsprint, a marker, paper, four red markers and a trash can. For each person you'll need a pencil, a copy of "The Acts of Prayer" handout (page 138), a Bible, and a copy of the "Prayer Journal" handout (page 140).

 # STARTING THE SESSION

Welcome everyone to the session. Have people sit in a circle. If you have more than 10 people, form small groups. Have people each sit with their hands folded in a traditional prayer position.

Then start with one person. Have him or her give an excuse not to pray, such as "I never hear God's voice" or "It seems like I'm talking to the ceiling," then lower his or her "praying hands" to point to someone else in the group. Give that person five seconds to think of another excuse and point to someone else. If someone doesn't think of an excuse in time, he or she is out. Continue playing until just one person is left.

On newsprint, have people list as many prayer hang-ups as they can think of based on the game and their experience. Then say: **We all have lots of questions about prayer and how to pray. These are the focus for this session as we search scripture for some answers to these questions.**

Remind people about the opening activity of "Spiritual Growth 1: Spiritual Gardening" (page 127) that compared the four food groups to four elements of a balanced spiritual diet. Then give some background about prayer, using information from the introduction to this session.

 # DIGGING INTO THE WORD

Give each person a pencil and a copy of "The Acts of Prayer" handout (page 138). Then assign each person one letter of the word "pray." Have young adults form different groups to study each part of the handout as follows:

● Adoration—Have young adults get together so everyone in the small group has a different letter. Each group will spell "pray."

● Confession—Have people get together with people who have the same letter—all P's together; all R's together, and so forth.

● Thanksgiving—All P's join with all R's, then form two equal groups; and all A's join with all Y's, then form two equal groups.

● Petition—All P's join with all Y's, then form two equal groups; all R's join with all A's, then form two equal groups.

If you have fewer than eight people, stay in one group for the activity.

Give groups time to work on the Adoration section of the handout, then have them rotate to the next group and set of questions. Continue until they've been through the whole handout.

Gather the whole group together, then ask:

● **Which type of prayer is most common? least common?**

● **Which type of prayer do you believe is most important?**

● **What experiences have you had with each type of prayer?**

APPLYING THE WORD

Say: **While it's important to study and talk about prayer, it's more important to pray. So we're going to spend time practicing the four elements of prayer. To do this, we'll use four different forms of prayer to show that prayer has many forms.**

Now have the group sit in a circle and lead young adults through each of the following types of prayer:

● Adoration using scripture meditation—Have everyone get comfortable, either standing or kneeling. Begin with a period of silence. Then have the class meditate on Psalm 89:1-18 by having different people read the Psalm aloud, one verse at a time. Pause between each verse.

● Confession using written prayer—Give each person paper and a pencil. Have them each write a personal prayer of confession. Ask people to put their confessions in the middle of the circle. Go to the center of the circle. As you pray aloud, thanking God for forgiveness, tear the confessions into tiny pieces and drop them in a trash can to symbolize forgiveness.

● Thanksgiving using "popcorn" prayer—Have group members each randomly call out words that indicate what they're thankful for. When the popping stops, have the whole class shout together, "Amen!"

● Petition using group prayer—Have people share their concerns with the whole group. Concerns may involve illness, personal struggles or challenges. Then join hands and pray together for each request. Close with a benediction.

AFFIRMING EACH OTHER

Read aloud James 5:13-16. Say: **Sometimes we think of prayer as something personal and private. And those are accurate descriptions in some cases. But prayer is also corporate— something we do together as Christians. Prayer is one way we support and encourage each other.**

Have people each find a partner. If you have an extra person, form one trio. Then have people each share with their partner something they'd like their partner to pray for them. It can be something spiritual, personal, work-related or family-related. Then have partners pray together and covenant to pray for each other through the coming week. This may be difficult for some who've never prayed aloud, but encourage them to participate.

CLOSING THE SESSION

Give each person a copy of the "Prayer Journal" handout (page 140). Encourage people to put what they've learned today into practice. Have them use the suggested format—or one that fits their prayer life—in a journal. Talk about the benefits of such a journal. Encourage people to bring their prayer journals to class to share any insights or concerns.

Close the session by praying The Lord's Prayer together.

THE ACTS OF PRAYER

Within your group, discuss the questions, read the passages and do the activities in your assigned category. Keep your notes on a separate piece of paper for future reference.

Adoration

1. Define adoration.

2. Read aloud Psalm 33:1-5. *How* is the Psalmist praising God? *What* is the Psalmist praising God for?

3. As a group, brainstorm characteristics or qualities of God for which you adore him. List your ideas on a piece of paper.

Confession

1. Define confession.

2. Read aloud 1 John 1:8-10. What does it mean to "confess your sins"? What does this verse say about God and prayer?

3. On a sheet of newsprint, work together for one minute to write—graffiti-style—as many sins as you can think of. Then using a red marker, write across the page "FORGIVEN." Talk about how loving God is to forgive sins we confess.

Thanksgiving

1. Define thanksgiving.

2. Read aloud 1 Thessalonians 5:18. What does this verse say about thanking God?

3. Beginning with one person in your group, thank someone else in the group for something. It can be anything. Then have that person thank someone else. Continue for one minute, making sure everyone is thanked at least once for something. Then talk about how it feels to say, "Thanks!" and how God might feel when we thank him.

Petition

1. Define petition.

2. Read aloud Matthew 7:7-12 and Hebrews 4:15-16. Why can we approach God with confidence? How does this relate to making requests to God?

3. Tear a piece of paper into enough pieces for each person in your group. Mark an "X" on one piece, then fold all the pieces so you can't tell which one has the X. Have each person take one. Then ask favors of each other, such as "Will you sit with me in church?" or "Can we get together sometime?" Everyone except the person with the X should give positive, affirming answers. But the person with the X must respond negatively to all comments. After talking for one minute, discuss what it would be like if God didn't take our requests seriously or always turned us down.

PRAYER JOURNAL

Keep a prayer journal and share with others what's happening in your prayer life. Using a spiral notebook, set up your personal prayer journal as follows—or in a different way that's more comfortable for you.

● Set aside one page for adoration. As you pray, list qualities and characteristics for which you adore God.

● Set aside another page for confession. As you pray, write what you've confessed. Then draw a dark line through it to symbolize how God has forgiven you.

● On a third page, write things you're thankful for. When those items involve other people, drop them a thank-you note too.

● Divide another page into four columns for requests or petitions using the following page setup:

Request Date	Prayer Request	Answer to Prayer	Answer Date

The Word on the Word

The Bible is the all-time best-selling book in the world.
Yet many of the people who own it leave it to collect dust
on a shelf. And that's not what God has in mind. The Bible is
meant to be read, studied and applied to our daily lives.

As young adults establish habits and patterns for adulthood,
it's a great time to nourish the habit of regular Bible study—one
of the four basic "spiritual food groups." This session reminds
young adults of the importance of Bible study, and it gives them
an opportunity to share their insights and preconceptions about
studying God's Word.

SURVEYING THE SESSION

This session focuses on learning to study the Bible. Young
adults will:

- play a game that reminds them what they know about
  the Bible;
- talk about the importance of the Bible and any
  preconceptions people have about it;
- share practical ways they've grown through Bible study;
  and
- encourage each other in Bible study.

UNDERSTANDING THE WORD

Scripture focus—Ephesians 6:13-17 and 2 Timothy 3:16-17.
The Bible passages for this session are scripture about
scripture—they give us insight about what the Bible is intended
to be.

Ephesians 6:13-17 describes the armor of God. One piece of that armor is the sword, which symbolizes God's Word. The imagery challenges Christians to prepare and protect themselves as they seek to live out their Christian beliefs in the world.

The 2 Timothy passage has raised significant debate among Christians about details of inspiration. However, the essence of the passage is clear. The Bible is God's Word and it was written to change people's lives.

PREPARING TO LEAD

Before the session, study the scripture passages listed in the Understanding the Word section. Then read the entire session outline. Make sure all the activities fit your group, and make any necessary changes.

Gather the materials for the session. You'll need paper, pencils, a die, newsprint, a marker, a stopwatch or watch, and tape. For each person you'll need a Bible, a pencil, three or four 3×5 cards and a copy of the "S.P.A.C.E. Study Card" (page 146).

STARTING THE SESSION

Welcome everyone to the session. Explain that this session is about Bible study, one of the four basic spiritual food groups. The other three food groups are prayer, fellowship and evangelism.

Form two teams to play Bible Picture Trivia. If you have more than 12 people in the class, form four teams and have two teams compete against each other so there are two competitions. Have paper, pencils and a die handy. Write the following key on newsprint:

1=Old Testament book;
2=New Testament book;
3=Old Testament character;
4=New Testament character;
5=Old Testament event or story; and
6=New Testament event or story.

Decide which team goes first. Then have one person on that team roll the die. Have him or her write an appropriate answer on a secret key, which you don't show anyone. Then have him or her use only pictures to convey the answer to his or her team.

For example, if someone rolled #2, he or she might write "Matthew" on the key. Then he or she could draw a doormat to imitate the sound of the first syllable or draw money as a clue to Matthew being a tax collector.

Using a stopwatch or watch, time the seconds it takes teams to guess. Keep a running score on how long each team takes.

When a team gets the answer correct, switch to the other team. Play at least until everyone on both teams has had a chance to roll and draw. Then total the times for all the answers and declare which team answered the questions in the shortest time.

 # DIGGING INTO THE WORD

Before digging into the Bible study, talk about people's preconceptions about the Bible. List key thoughts on newsprint.
Ask:
● **If someone on the street asked you why the Bible is important or holy, what would you say?**
● **Why don't many Christians read the Bible?**
● **What's hardest about studying the Bible?**
Then read aloud 2 Timothy 3:16-17.
Ask:
● **What does it mean that scripture is inspired by God? How does that affect your attitude toward the Bible?**
● **What's the goal of scripture as listed in verse 17? How have you seen scripture fulfill this goal in your life?**
On separate sheets of newsprint, write the four ways verse 16 says studying scripture is profitable: teaching, rebuking, correcting and training in righteousness. Tape each sheet to separate walls in your room. Then have people each go to each sheet and write one experience they've had when scripture has helped them in this way. For example, someone might write on the

"rebuking" sheet, "Bible study helped me learn that my lifestyle was too materialistic."

If people can't think of examples, have them write questions or personal hang-ups about the category. For example, someone might write on the "rebuking" sheet, "It's hard for me to see this as a benefit because I've seen it misused to hurt people so much." Encourage people to be honest with their answers and questions.

When everyone has written on each sheet, go around the room and discuss stories, insights, questions and hang-ups. Be careful not to criticize or put people on the spot. Instead, have people talk about their feelings, frustrations and successes.

Read aloud Ephesians 6:13-17. Note that the passage shows imagery of a Christian preparing for spiritual battle. All the pieces of armor listed are defensive, except one.

Have students identify the sword—the Word—as the offensive piece of armor. Then ask:

● **How is the Bible like a sword? unlike a sword?**

● **What kind of spiritual battles do you face that require a sword?**

● **Can a sword ever be used inappropriately? What parallels do you see between the appropriate use of a sword and appropriate use of scripture?**

● **Often fencers—those who duel with swords—improve their skills by fencing with each other. How can we help each other prepare for "battle" in terms of studying and using the Bible?**

APPLYING THE WORD

Say: **Scripture won't make a difference in our lives if we don't read and study it. But sometimes we have questions about how to approach Bible study.**

Give people each a pencil and three or four 3×5 cards. Have them each write on their card questions about how to study the Bible. Encourage them to be specific. Explain that you'll collect the cards and read them without identifying the writer. Then have other people in the class share ideas of what has worked for them.

After people write questions, collect and shuffle the cards. Then read the questions one by one, giving people time to offer their suggestions. If several cards have similar questions, spend more time on those since more people are interested. Keep the discussion focused on practical ways to get into regular and helpful Bible study.

 ## AFFIRMING EACH OTHER

Use this affirmation time to encourage each other in Bible study. Form a circle. Have a Bible ready. Say: **We've talked a lot about how Bible study can help us grow spiritually. Now we're going to symbolize our support for each other by passing around this Bible.**

As leader, begin the process. Hand the Bible to the person on your left and say, "I commend God's Word to you, (name), as you seek to _____." Mention a specific area you know that person wants to work on, such as finding God's will or deepening personal prayer life. Continue around the circle until the Bible returns to you.

 ## CLOSING THE SESSION

Close the session by reading aloud Joshua 1:8—a passage with a promise about the value of studying God's Word. Encourage people to share insights they gain from the passage. Ask people to share ways they've been "prosperous and successful" through studying the Bible.

Then suggest that group members read a chapter per day in the Gospel of John this week. Give them each a copy of the "S.P.A.C.E. Study Card" (page 146) to guide them. Encourage them to look for the themes listed on the card as they read and to keep track of them in a Bible study journal.

S.P.A.C.E. STUDY CARD

Look for these themes—which form the acronym SPACE—to guide you as you study the Bible. Record your discoveries in a Bible study journal.

Sins to confess.
Promises to keep.
Actions to avoid.
Commands to obey.
Examples to follow.

The Locker Room and Playing Field

It's a tough, tough game. Mud, sweat and blood have combined to give you the look of the villain in a B-grade horror movie. You're tired. The other team seems almost invincible. But the score is still close.

And then it's halftime. You retreat into the sanctuary of the locker room. Warm. Inviting. Refreshing. Fresh uniforms. A wise, encouraging coach who explains the strategy for the second half. Motivational. Instructional. Powerful. And your fellow teammates, cheering each other on.

Your attitude and mood have changed.

But you can't stay in the locker room forever. "Three minutes 'til game time!" the official yells. And you charge through the tunnel to play.

This final session on spiritual growth is about the locker room and the playing field. The locker room represents fellowship. The playing field represents evangelism—sharing your faith.

We prepare to play in the locker room of Christian fellowship. But we must leave the locker room to share our faith on the "playing field." Without the encouragement of the locker room, the field would seem too hostile and foreboding. Without the playing field, the locker room would be wasted. The two go together.

SURVEYING THE SESSION

This session looks at the "spiritual foods" of fellowship and evangelism. Young adults will:

● create symbols of Christian fellowship;

- participate in an activity to illustrate the dangers of exclusive Christian fellowship;
- study scripture that challenges Christians to be in fellowship and to share their faith;
- do role plays of different witnessing styles;
- evaluate the balance of fellowship and evangelism in their group; and
- affirm each other with notes.

UNDERSTANDING THE WORD

Scripture focus—John 17:20-21; Acts 1:8; 2:42-47; and 4:12; Romans 1:16; 3:23; and 6:23; Galatians 1:6-9; Ephesians 6:19-20; Hebrews 10:24-25; and James 5:16.

This session surveys a wide variety of passages that deal with fellowship and evangelism. Themes in the passages include:

- Christians should be united in fellowship.
- Jesus calls all followers to be witnesses in the world.
- Being a Christian naturally involves being in fellowship with other Christians.
- Salvation is through Christ alone.
- Christians should share the gospel proudly and fearlessly.
- Christians should encourage each other to grow in faith and should support each other in prayer.

 PREPARING TO LEAD

Before the session, study the passages listed in the Understanding the Word section. Then read the entire session outline. Make sure all the activities fit your group, and make any necessary changes.

Gather the materials for the session. For every three people, you'll need a handful of gumdrops and a box of toothpicks. You'll need newsprint, a marker, the "Giving It Away" strips (page 154), and a box or basket. For each person you'll need a Bible, newsprint, markers, a copy of the "Which Witness Wins?"

handout (page 153), a pencil, three blank telegrams or three 3×5 cards, and three envelopes.

STARTING THE SESSION

Welcome everyone to the last session in the series. Remind people of the two "spiritual food groups" you've studied: prayer and Bible study. Then mention you'll be studying the remaining two in this session: fellowship and evangelism.

Form trios. Give each trio a handful of gumdrops and a box of toothpicks. Ask them each to design a gumdrop-and-toothpick creation that symbolizes Christian fellowship.

Allow five minutes, then ask each group to explain its creation.

Ask:

● **What feelings do you have when you think of Christian fellowship?**

● **How does Christian fellowship differ from other relationships?**

● **How does fellowship help you spiritually?**

DIGGING INTO THE WORD

When they've finished, have everyone stand in a circle. If you have more than 10 people, form small groups of no more than 10 each. Assign one person to be the "outsider," and have him or her step out of the circle.

Then tell the remaining members to form as tight a circle as possible—arms around each other like a football huddle. Have them do everything they can to keep the outsider from getting into the circle. The circle can whirl, move and do anything else necessary to keep the outsider out. The outsider can do anything to get in—except stand on a chair or table and dive over the insiders.

Give the signal and let the contest begin. Periodically choose a new outsider so different people experience what it's

Ask the outsiders:
- **How did it feel trying to get in?**
- **What methods did you use? Which ones worked?**
- **How did you feel about the people in the circle?**

Ask the insiders:
- **How did it feel to keep someone out?**
- **How did you feel about the outsider?**
- **How did you feel about others in the circle?**

Ask everyone:
- **When, if ever, have you felt like an outsider when visiting a church?**
- **When, if ever, have you felt like the insider keeping others out?**
- **How is our church similar to or different from this game?**

Ask volunteers to read aloud each of the following passages:

- John 17:20-21
- Hebrews 10:24-25
- Acts 2:42-47
- James 5:16

After each passage, have people indicate the truths about fellowship they see in the passage. Jot the ideas on newsprint.

When they've finished, move to the material on sharing your faith. Introduce the subject by briefly sharing the sports analogy used in the introduction to the session.

Have people form groups of four for a role-play exercise. If you have extra people, have them join another group and double up the roles. Then give each person a copy of the "Which Witness Wins?" handout (page 153). Have people each choose a role from the handout, then spend about five minutes acting their roles.

Then bring all the groups together in a circle.

Ask:
- **Which roles were most comfortable? least comfortable?**
- **What were the strengths and weaknesses of each witness?**
- **When have you seen people live these roles? What happened?**

Form pairs. If you have an extra person, form one trio. Give each pair one of the strips from the "Giving It Away" handout (page 154). If you have fewer than five pairs, give some pairs more than one strip. If you have more than 10 people, make duplicate strips and give the same strip to two or more pairs.

Have pairs read their scripture and discuss each question or questions. When they're ready, bring everyone together. Have pairs each read aloud their passage and report on their discussion.

To pull together the two themes of fellowship and evangelism, ask:

● **What's the relationship between fellowship and evangelism?**

● **What happens when a Christian or church focuses only on fellowship and forgets evangelism?**

● **What happens when a Christian or church focuses only on evangelism and forgets fellowship?**

 ## APPLYING THE WORD

Set up a continuum in your room. Explain that one wall represents "evangelism only." The opposite wall represents "fellowship only." Have people stand somewhere between the two walls to indicate where they feel your group is along this continuum. No one may stand exactly in the middle.

As people stand in place, ask:

● **Are you comfortable with where you're standing on the continuum?**

● **Do you feel your group has a balance of evangelism and fellowship? Why or why not?**

● **If you don't think your group is balanced, what steps could we take to help our church move to a more balanced position?**

List ideas from the last question on newsprint. Encourage people each to focus on things they can do. Discuss any specific strategies your group might want to employ to get the process going.

Affirming Each Other

Give each person a pencil, three blank telegrams or three 3×5 cards, and three envelopes. At the top of each telegram or card, have people each write their first and last name. Then collect the telegrams in a box or basket.

Now have people each draw from the box three telegrams or cards. If they draw one of their own, have them put it back and draw another. Tell them not to say whose cards they have.

Then ask people each to write a short "telegram" to the person on the card, telling him or her why they enjoy being part of the Christian community with that person. Then have them place each telegram or card in an envelope and write the person's name on the outside.

Collect all the telegrams when everyone is finished. Deliver the telegrams to each addressee. Give people time to read the notes silently.

Closing the Session

Have people stand in a circle and face inward. Lead in prayer, asking God to help your group and church grow in Christian fellowship and love.

Then have people turn around so everyone is facing outward. Continue the prayer, asking God to help people take the nourishment, encouragement and support they receive through Christian fellowship and share the good news with others.

WHICH WITNESS WINS?

Have each person in your group choose one of the following characters to role-play:

Ron or Rhonda Regular—This character is an average person who's interested in knowing more about this "Christian thing." He or she isn't hostile, but is skeptical.

Betty or Bill Bible—This Christian sees witnessing as reciting one Bible verse after another—mostly verses on damnation and what happens if you don't repent. He or she is very graphic.

Ralph or Rose Relational—This Christian's faith is purely personal. He or she has no idea how anyone else can become a believer. This person doesn't ever refer to the Bible in telling others what it means to follow Christ. He or she only talks on the feeling level.

Nancy or Ned Non-commital—This person has so many questions about theology that he or she is reluctant to talk about faith. He or she is afraid someone might ask a tough question. What kind of witness would it be if he or she couldn't answer the question?

Have Ron or Rhonda begin the conversation with a non-committal inquiry about Christianity or church. Then have each character respond. Ron or Rhonda can ask lots of questions.

GIVING IT AWAY

Cut apart these strips so each pair has at least one strip.

- - - ✂ -

Read Romans 3:23 and 6:23. What's the basic message when you put these two verses together?

- - - ✂ -

Read Acts 4:12 and Galatians 1:6-9. What's the main message of these passages?

- - - ✂ -

Read Romans 1:16. What are some reasons we act ashamed of Jesus? Are these reasons good reasons? Why or why not?

- - - ✂ -

Read Ephesians 6:19-20. What did Paul do when he had fears about proclaiming Christ? How can we apply this in our own lives?

- - - ✂ -

Read Acts 1:8. What part does the Holy Spirit play in us sharing our faith? What does it mean to be a witness?

- - - ✂ -

Bring Active Learning Into Your Adult Education Classrooms!

APPLY-IT-TO-LIFE™ ADULT BIBLE SERIES OFFERS ADULT GROUPS...

- ACTIVE LEARNING!

  Apply-It-To-Life™ Adult Bible Series teaches as Jesus taught—with *active learning*. Participants get involved in experiences and learn to share with others in the group—rather than listening to a lecture.

- REAL LIFE ISSUES!

  Lessons help connect scriptural truths to real life. Then, through group interaction, discovery, and discussion, adults will...
    - learn from each other's experiences how to grow closer to God,
    - dig into the Scriptures and come away with a personal application of the passages,
    - explore how God works through relationships, and
    - learn what it means to be a Christian in today's world.

- NO STUDENT BOOKS—EASY FOR TEACHERS!

  Each **Apply-It-To-Life** topic is covered in four lessons. Change the topic after four weeks, or mix and match other titles in the series to provide your class with a variety of challenging and interesting topics. Everything you need for any-size class is included to make your job a breeze: complete leaders guide, handout masters you can photocopy, publicity helps, and bonus ideas. Plus, your teaching commitment is only four weeks!

- LOW COST!

  Because there are no student books to buy, the cost per adult is minimal—and the books can be used over and over, year after year! Offer classes the adults in your church will enjoy—and save money at the same time!

  Put your adult education in a new direction—order **Apply-It-To-Life Adult Bible Series** today!

The Church: What Am I Doing Here?	ISBN 1-55945-294-3
Communication: Enhancing Your Relationships	ISBN 1-55945-297-8
Evangelism for Every Day	ISBN 1-55945-298-6
Faith in the Workplace	ISBN 1-55945-299-4
Marriage: Choosing a Lifetime Partner	ISBN 1-55945-296-X
Revelation: Unlocking Its Secrets	ISBN 1-55945-295-1

Order today from your local Christian bookstore, or write: Group Publishing, Box 485, Loveland, CO 80539. For mail orders, please add postage/handling of $4 for orders up to $15, $5 for orders of $15.01+. Colorado residents add 3% sales tax.

Your Group Won't Stop Talking—Guaranteed!

Get your kids and adults really talking with this exciting new video series complete with leaders guide. Each hot topic is guaranteed to start discussions and motivate your viewers to explore Scripture for answers to their tough, thought-provoking questions. All segments are real—not staged or acted out.

The video format makes for easy use. Preview the appropriate video and Leaders Guide section before using with your group. Then, follow the suggested format to get the most out of each segment with your group...
- open the meeting with one of the openers listed;
- work through the exercises included;
- play the segment of the tape to your group;
- use the Leaders Guide to encourage the conversations that develop; and
- close by choosing one of the closing options listed.

The leaders guide also helps prepare you to deal with the conversations that develop. Information for each video segment includes...
- meeting plans for each topic,
- appropriate Scripture to guide biblical conversations,
- lesson objectives,
- photocopiable handouts to get your group involved in the lesson, and
- statistics and other tips that support the segment topic.

Don't waste another meeting in silence. Start your group talking with Group's **Hot Talk-Starter Videos**.

SERIES 1
Teen Suicide•An Atheist's Beliefs•Dating: He Says/She Says•Teenagers in the KKK
ISBN 1-55945-259-5

SERIES 2
Pregnant Teenager•R-Rated Movies•What's a Monk?•Hooked on Gambling
ISBN 1-55945-274-9

SERIES 3
The Rapture of 1992 (Part 1)•The Rapture of 1992 (Part 2)•Underage Smoker•A Visit to a New Age Store•The Gang Life
ISBN 1-55945-275-7

SERIES 4
Gay Rights•Palm Reading•Body Image: Glamour Shots•Homeless Teenagers
ISBN 1-55945-276-5

Hot Talk-Starter Set (all four series)
ISBN 1-55945-277-3

WARNING: These video programs deal with sensitive issues and do not supply conclusions. Preview segments before use. Prepare your discussion leaders using the accompanying guide. Use these presentations only when accompanied by a careful debriefing time.
